GW00602839

# Certificate  Paper 6

# The Audit Framework

First edition April 1995

ISBN 0 7517 0105 X

**British Library Cataloguing-in-Publication Data**

A catalogue record for this book
is available from the British Library

Published by

BPP Publishing Limited
Aldine House, Aldine Place
London W12 8AW

Printed in Great Britain by
Ashford Colour Press, Gosport, Hampshire

All our rights reserved. No part of this publication may
be reproduced, stored in a retrieval system or
transmitted, in any form or by any means, electronic,
mechanical, photocopying, recording or otherwise,
without the prior written permission of BPP Publishing
Limited.

©
BPP Publishing Limited
1995

*PASSCARDS* are a new study and revision aid from BPP, designed specifically both to *save you time* and *increase your chances of passing*.

- They present the key facts in an easily digestible form.
  - These key facts will help to bring back to mind the detail you have learnt from the BPP Study Text.

- There are plenty of diagrams: each one will kick-start your memory on a key topic.
  - The diagrams are backed up by clear revision notes.

- You will also find *exam hints* scattered throughout the cards, giving those little pointers which can make all the difference.

- The cards are pocket sized, so you can fit in a quick revision session on the bus or the train each morning.

- This pack of cards follows the structure of the BPP Study Text. Groups of cards correspond to chapters in the Text.

We suggest that you run through the complete set of cards once a fortnight in the run-up to the exam, to keep the subject fresh in your mind and to remind yourself that you actually do know quite a lot. Finally, on the night before the exam, look again at all of the diagrams. This will put you in the best possible position to achieve exam success. Good luck!

Page

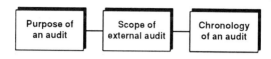

## Purpose of an audit

'An audit is the independent examination of, and expression of an opinion on, the financial statements of an enterprise.'

CA 1985 requires the directors of all companies to produce financial statements for presentation to their shareholders. This is a recognition of the division between those who own the company - the shareholders - and those who run it on a day-to-day basis - the directors. The directors are required to account for the stewardship of the assets placed under their control.

An audit is another legal requirement. The directors' financial statements have to be examined by an independent expert - the auditor who is required to give an opinion on their truth and fairness. His role is therefore to report to the shareholders on the degree of reliance they should place on the financial statements presented by the directors.

Other people may also like to see the financial statements. They will use them as a basis for assessing the state of the company and as such they are also interested in the audit report.

- Potential shareholders/investors
- Lenders
- Employees
- Analysts
- Business advisers
- Customers/suppliers
- Government

## Scope of external audit

### Statutory audits

These are required by CA 1985 for companies; also, various other bodies need an audit under different legislation, eg building societies under the Building Societies Act 1965.

### Non-statutory audits

These are performed on various clubs, charities, sole traders and partnerships because the owners, members etc want one, not because it is required by law. There are various advantages to such audits, particularly the acceptance of accounts by the Inland Revenue.

### Small companies

Small companies may not need an audit if the managers and owners of the business are the same people. This is discussed further in Chapter 12.

### External vs internal audit

Larger organisations may have their own internal audit department. Internal auditors act as an additional control and their work can be of direct benefit to the external auditor as discussed in Chapter 25.

## Chronology of an audit

The following (simplified) diagram represents an audit approach based on the *Operational Standard* (see Chapter 2).

---

*Exam hint*. Learn this diagram.

---

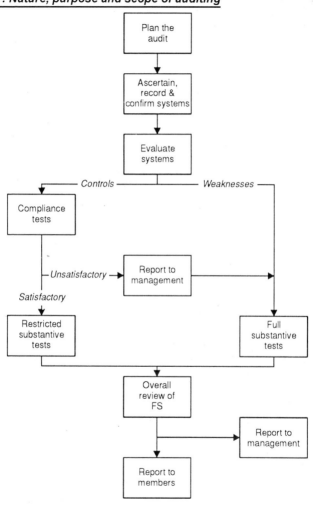

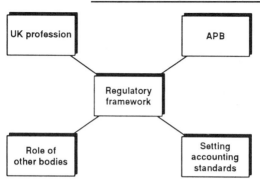

## UK profession

There are a large number of accountancy bodies in the UK, eg ACCA, ICAEW, CIMA etc. They all vary from each other in certain ways, but all are characterised by:

- Stringent entrance requirements
- Codes of ethics and behaviour
- Maintenance standards through technical update

The current regulation over the auditing side of the profession was introduced by CA 1989 amendments to CA 1985.

### *Recognised Qualifying Bodies (RQBs)*

RQBs must offer a qualification in accountancy together with rules on:

- Admission to or expulsion from a course of study leading to a qualification

- Award or deprivation of a qualification

- Approval of a person for the purposes of giving practical training

*Recognised Supervisory Bodies (RSBs)*

Bodies established in the UK which maintain and enforce rules as to:

- Eligibility of persons to seek appointment as company auditor

- Conduct of company audit work

This legislation brought UK legislation into line with the EU 8th Directive on company law. This requires that persons carrying out statutory audits must be approved by the authorities of EU member states, the authority in the UK being delegated to Recognised Supervisory Bodies (RSBs). One of the RSBs is the ACCA.

RSBs are required to have rules to ensure that persons eligible for appointment as a company auditor are either:

- Individuals holding an appropriate qualification, or
- Firms controlled by qualified persons

A number of other requirements concern the procedures which RSBs must follows to maintain the competence of members.

- Ensure that only 'fit and proper' persons are appointed as company auditors (exams, post qualification experience)

- Ensure that company audit work is conducted properly and with 'professional integrity' (Rules of Professional Conduct)

- Include rules as to the technical standards of company audit work (presumably this means auditing standards and guidelines, although the Act does not state this)

- Ensure that eligible persons maintain an 'appropriate level of competence' (CPE, Monitoring Unit)

- Ensure that all firms eligible under its rules have arrangements to prevent:

- o Individuals not holding an appropriate qualification, and
- o Persons who are not members of the firm from being able to exert influence over an audit which would be likely to affect the independence or integrity of the audit

The RSB's rules must provide for adequate monitoring and enforcement of compliance with its rules and must include provisions relating to:

- Admission and expulsion of members
- Investigation of complaints against members
- Compulsory professional indemnity insurance

Professional qualifications, which will be prerequisites for membership of an RSB, will be offered by RQBs approved by the Secretary of State.

Up-to-date lists of approved auditors' names and addresses are maintained by the RSBs; this register must be made available to the public.

The RSBs and their officers etc, are exempt from damages in respect of any action arising out of the exercise of their statutory duties, unless they have acted in bad faith.

*Eligibility/ineligibility*

Membership of an RSB is the main prerequisite for eligibility to act as an auditor. CA 1989 also allows a 'firm' (partnership or body corporate) to be appointed as a company auditor.

Under CA 1985, a person is *ineligible* for appointment as a company auditor if he or she is:

- An officer or employee of the company
- A partner or employee of such a person
- A partnership in which such a person is a partner

- Ineligible by virtue of any of the above for appointment as auditor of any parent or subsidiary undertaking or a subsidiary undertaking of any parent undertaking of the company, or

- There exists between him or her or any associate (or his or hers) and the company (or a company as referred to above) a connection of any description as may be specified in regulations laid down by Secretary of State

This does not disqualify a shareholder or debtor/creditor of the company, or a close relative of an officer/employee, but these would be excluded by the relevant RSB.

Ineligibility may also arise through 'lack of independence'.

If during his term of office a company auditor becomes ineligible for appointment to the office, he must vacate office and give notice in writing to the company.

**APB**

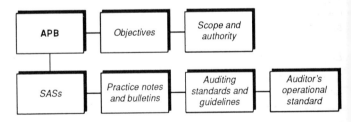

Established in 1991 by the Consultative Committee of Accountancy Bodies (CCAB) to advance standards of auditing and associated review activities and to provide a framework of practice for exercise of the auditors' role.

In addition to practising auditors, members of the APB include persons from the business and academic worlds, the public sector and the legal profession. The APB has up to 18 voting members and not more than 5 non-voting members. The Chairman and up to 8 other voting members are required to be practising auditors.

*Objectives*

The APB is committed to leading the development of auditing practice in the UK so as to:

- Establish high standards of auditing
- Meet the developing needs of users of financial information
- Ensure public confidence in the auditing process

To achieve these objectives, the APB intends to:

- Take an active role in the development of statutes, regulations and accounting standards which affect the audit profession

- Promote ways of increasing the value of audits and of ensuring their cost effectiveness

- Consult with the users of financial information to ensure that the APB provides an effective and timely response to their developing needs and to issues raised by them

- Advance the wider public's understanding of the roles and responsibilities of auditors

- Establish and publish statements of the principles and procedures with which auditors are required to comply in the conduct of audits, and other explanatory material to assist in their interpretation and application; pronouncements will have due regard to international developments

*Scope and authority*

There are 3 types of APB pronouncement: Statements of Auditing Standards (SASs), Practice Notes and Bulletins.

As well as financial statements, audit and related service engagements may involve other financial information, or non-financial information such as:

- Adequacy of internal control systems

- Compliance with statutory, regulatory or contractual requirements

- Economy, efficiency and effectiveness in the use of resources ('value-for-money' auditing)

- Environmental practices

The APB recognises the fundamental importance of *professional judgement* being applied by auditors in all audit and other engagements. The pronouncements of the APB give a *framework* to support and assist auditors.

*SASs*

The *scope* of SASs is as follows.

- SASs contain *basic principles* and *essential procedures* (Auditing Standards), indicated by bold type, with which auditors are required to comply, except where otherwise stated in the SAS concerned, in the conduct of any audit of financial statements

- In addition to SASs of general application the APB issues SASs containing additional Auditing Standards applicable to the conduct of audits of *certain types* of entity

- SASs also include *explanatory* and other material which, rather than being prescriptive, is designed to assist auditors in interpreting and apply Auditing Standards

- Auditing Standards need not be applied to matters whose effect is in the auditors' judgement not material

The *authority* of SASs is as follows.

- Members of CCAB have undertaken to adopt all SASs promulgated by the APB; apparent failures by auditors to comply with the Auditing Standards contained within SASs are liable to be enquired into by the relevant accountancy body, and disciplinary or regulatory action may result

- Auditors who do *not* comply with Auditing Standards when performing company or other audits make themselves liable to regulatory action by their RSB, which may include the withdrawal of registration and hence of eligibility to perform company audits

- All APB pronouncements and in particular Auditing Standards are likely to be taken into account when the adequacy of the work of auditors is being considered in a court of law or in other contested situations

In the *development* of SASs, the APB is committed to wide consultation. Prior to issuing SASs, the APB issues exposure drafts for general public and specialist comment. The approval of at least three quarters of the voting members of the APB is required before an SAS can be issued.

*Practice Notes and Bulletins*

The APB also issues:

- Practice Notes, to assist auditors in applying Auditing Standards of general application to particular circumstances and industries

- Bulletins, to provide auditors with timely guidance on new or emerging issues

Practice Notes and Bulletins are:

- Persuasive rather than prescriptive
- Indicative of good practice
- Of similar status to the explanatory material in SASs

Bulletins may be developed into SASs or Practice Notes; some Practice Notes may be developed into SASs.

*Auditing Standards and Guidelines*

The APB has adopted the Auditing Standards and Guidelines prepared by its predecessor body, the APC, and these remain in force until withdrawn or replaced by SASs or Practice Notes. The old Auditing Standards and the new Auditing Standards contained within SASs have the same status. Auditing Guidelines have the same status as Practice Notes.

*Auditor's Operational Standard*

Only one of the APC's two Auditing Standards remains extant. The *Operational Standard* gives the basic plan for every audit and each of its five points is backed up by an operational guideline.

---

*Exam hint.* You should *learn* the contents of the *Operational Standard*

---

**The Auditor's Operational Standard**

1   *Planning, controlling and recording*

    The auditor should adequately *plan, control* and *record* his
    work.

2   *Accounting systems*

    The auditor should *ascertain* the enterprise's *system* of
    recording and processing transactions and *assess its adequacy*
    as a basis for the preparation of financial statements.

3   *Audit evidence*

    The auditor should obtain *relevant* and *reliable audit evidence
    sufficient* to enable him to draw reasonable conclusions
    therefrom.

4   *Internal controls*

    *If the auditor wishes to place reliance on any internal controls*,
    he should *ascertain* and *evaluate* those controls and *perform
    compliance tests* on their operation.

5   *Review of financial statements*

    The auditor should carry out such a *review* of the financial
    statements as is sufficient, in conjunction with the conclusions
    drawn from the other audit evidence obtained, *to give him a
    reasonable basis for his opinion* on the financial statements.

You can see the relationship between the above and the
diagram at the end of Chapter 1.

## Setting accounting standards

*Standard setting regime*

You should be aware of the standard setting process and the relationship between auditing and accounting. The standard setting and enforcement regime is as follows.

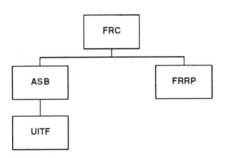

- *Financial Reporting Council* oversees whole process, makes appointments, ensures funding etc

- *Financial Reporting Review Panel* examines annual reports etc to look at departures from accounting standards

- *Accounting Standards Board* produces new FRSs (from FREDs and sometimes DDs) and other related documents

- *Urgent Issues Task Force* tackles important matters as they arise

Auditing and accounting are closely connected at many levels. In particular, there are some formal connections which arise between accounting (in a financial reporting sense) and auditing.

- The auditor of a company must report if a company has not followed an accounting standard in preparing its accounts

- When accounting standards are implemented in company accounts, they will give comfort that the accounts show a true and fair view; of great importance to the auditor

*Statement of Principles*

You should be aware of the contents of the *Statement of Principles*. All 7 chapters have now been published as DDs or FREDs.

1  Objectives of financial statements
2  Qualitative characteristics of financial information
3  Elements of financial statements
4  Recognition of items in financial statements
5  Presentation of financial information
6  Valuation and measurement
7  The reporting entity

## Role of other bodies

- *Government*
  - Companies Act legislation (as seen above)
  - DTI investigations, papers etc
  - Other regulators, eg SIB
  - Office of Fair Trading and MMC

- *International bodies*
  - EU directives
  - International Auditing Practices Committee (IAPC) and International Standards on Auditing (ISAs)

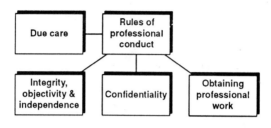

## Due care

The standard of work of an *accountant* is generally defined by the Supply of Goods and Services Act 1982.

The standard of work required of an *auditor of a limited company* is not defined in CA 1985. Various judgements in cases have attempted to define the auditor's duty of care, and these can be summarised as follows.

- General rules in law lay down auditor's duties (see Chapter 24), as may the auditor's terms of appointment

- What is 'reasonable skill, care and caution' will depend on the individual facts in each particular case

- Account will be taken of auditing standards when considering the adequacy of the auditor's work (see above)

- If the auditor's suspicions are aroused then he or she should investigate to a greater extent

*Summary*: it is the duty of the auditor to employ reasonable care in all he or she does.

## Rules of Professional Conduct

These rules lay out the professional ethics and behaviour required by members *and* students of the ACCA. Guidance is in the form of:

- Fundamental principles
- Statements
- Explanatory notes

*Fundamental principles*

Members should:

- Behave with integrity in all professional, business and personal financial relationships. Integrity implies not merely honesty but fair dealing and truthfulness

- Strive for objectivity in all professional and business judgements. Objectivity is the state of mind which has regard to all considerations relevant to the task in hand but no other. It presupposes intellectual honesty

- Not accept or perform work which they are not competent to undertake unless they obtain such advice and assistance as will enable them competently to carry out the work

- Carry out their professional work with due skill, care, diligence and expedition and with proper regard for the technical and professional standards expected of them as members

- Behave with courtesy and consideration towards all with whom they come into contact during the course of performing their work

*Specific guidance statements*

These indicate those areas where members should be aware that there may be problems in the application of the fundamental principles.

1   Integrity, objectivity and independence (see below)
2   The professional duty of confidence
3   Obtaining professional work (see below)
4   Practice names and descriptions
5   Changes in professional appointments (see Chapter 7)
6   Ownership of books and papers
7   Retention of books, files, working papers and other documents
8   Activities through corporate or non-corporate organisations
9   Fees
11  Professional liability of accountants and auditors
13  The incapacity or death of a sole practitioner
14  Clients' monies
17  Financial Services Act 1986
19  Disciplinary action in respect of convictions before the Courts
22  Corporate finance advice including takeovers
23  Confidentiality (see below)
24  The names of practising firms
25  Conflicts of interest
26  The ethical responsibilities of member in business

## Integrity, objectivity and independence

> A member's objectivity must be beyond question if he or she is to report as an auditor. That objectivity can only be assured if the member is, and is seen to be, independent.

- Undue dependence on an audit client: audit fees and other recurring work as % of gross fee income:
  - < 15% for client/group connected clients
  - < 10% for public interest companies
  - new clients: consider if >5-15%

- Overdue fees
- Actual/threatened litigation
- Associated firms: influences outside the practice
- Family and other personal relationships
  - 'Closely connected' client/auditor not allowed (adult child, spouse, siblings and spouses, financially assisted relative)
  - Senior audit staff greater threat than junior
  - Threat reduced if not on audit/at separate office/effective safeguards

- Beneficial interest in shares or other investments
- Trusts
- Voting an audit appointment
- Loans to and from clients
  - Practice loans prohibited
  - Individual loans OK if normal commercial terms

- Goods, services and hospitality (unless modest)
- Provision of other services to audit client
  - Acceptable to provide additional services
  - Should not perform executive functions
  - Preparation of accounts allowed for private companies but not public
  - Auditor cannot be officer/employee of the company, now or for the two years before first day of accounting period

Aids to independence; proposals include:

- Rotation of auditors
- State auditing board
- Audit committees
- Peer reviews
- Appointment by government

## Confidentiality

- *Improper disclosure*: only disclose confidential information where permission obtained or right or duty to disclose

- *Improper use of information:* such information should not be used for auditor's/third party's personal gain

## Obtaining professional work

- Should not obtain/seek work in an unprofessional manner

- Can advertise but should have regard to relevant advertising codes and standards

- Do not make disparaging references to or comparisons with the services of others

- Should not quote fees without great care not to mislead as to precise range of services and time commitment that fees are intended to cover, but can offer free consultations to discuss level of fees

- No 'cold calling'

- Direct mailing permitted (ie material can be sent to non-clients provided no follow-up by phone/visit)

- No fees/commission or reward to third parties in return for introduction of clients

- No harassment of prospective clients

---

*Exam hint.* You may be asked to apply the above Rules to 'real life' situations in the exam. As well as using the Rules for guidance, you should also use your professional *common sense*. Avoid extreme reactions.

---

## Auditor's report

The auditor's report communicates a direct message to the shareholder or other reader of the financial statements, that the components of the accounts examined by the auditor show a true and fair view. It is the 'end product' of the audit.

### Unqualified audit report

SAS 600 aims to close the 'expectations gap' to some extent by extending the audit report and clarifying the respective responsibilities of the auditors and the directors.

SAS 600 states that the audit report should state clearly:

- The addressee

- The financial statements audited

- Separate sections, appropriately headed, dealing with:
    - Respective responsibilities of directors and auditors
    - The basis of the auditors' opinion
    - The auditors' opinion on the financial statements

- The identity of the auditor

- The date of the report

- Any other information or opinions prescribed by statutory or other requirements

An example of an unqualified report is as follows.

AUDITORS' REPORT TO THE SHAREHOLDERS OF XYZ PLC

We have audited the financial statements on pages ... to ... which have been prepared under the historical cost convention (as modified by the revaluation of certain fixed assets) and the accounting policies set out on page .... .

*Respective responsibilities of directors and auditors*
As described on page ... the company's directors are responsible for the preparation of financial statements. It is our responsibility to form an independent opinion, based on our audit, on those statements and to report our opinion to you.

*Basis of opinion*
We conducted our audit in accordance with Auditing Standards issued by the Auditing Practices Board. An audit includes examination, on a test basis, of evidence relevant to the amounts and disclosures in the financial statements. It also includes an assessment of the significant estimates and judgements made by the directors in the preparation of the financial statements, and of whether the accounting policies are appropriate to the company's circumstances, consistently applied and adequately disclosed.

We planned and performed our audit so as to obtain all the information and explanations which we considered necessary in order to provide us with sufficient evidence to give reasonable assurance that the financial statements are free from material misstatement, whether caused by fraud or other irregularity or error. In forming our opinion we also evaluated the overall adequacy of the presentation of information in the financial statements.

*Opinion*
In our opinion the financial statements give a true and fair view of the state of the company's affairs as at 31 December 19..

and of its profit (loss) for the year then ended and have been properly prepared in accordance with the Companies Act 1985.

*Registered auditors*                                                        *Address*
*Date*

The description of directors' responsibilities makes clear their responsibility to prepare financial statements and in doing so:

- To select suitable accounting policies and then apply them consistently

- To make judgements and estimates that are reasonable and prudent

- To state whether applicable accounting standards have been followed, subject to any material departures disclosed and explained in the financial statements (large companies only)

- To prepare the financial statements on the going concern basis unless it is inappropriate to presume that the company will continue in business (if no separate statement on going concern is made by the directors)

The directors' responsibilities for keeping proper accounting records, for safeguarding the assets of the company and hence for the prevention and detection of fraud and other irregularities are also made clear.

An unqualified opinion on financial statements is expressed when in the auditors' judgement they give a true and fair view and have been prepared in accordance with relevant accounting or other requirements. This judgement entails concluding whether *inter alia*:

- The financial statements have been prepared using appropriate accounting policies, which have been consistently applied

- The financial statements have been prepared in accordance with relevant legislation, regulations or applicable accounting standards (and that any departures are justified and adequately explained in the financial statements), and

- There is adequate disclosure of all information relevant to the proper understanding of the financial statements.

---

*Exam hint*. One method of examining the audit report would be to provide you with a copy of an unqualified audit report, with certain phrases underlined, and ask you to explain the meaning of certain highlighted phrases and justify their inclusion.

---

## Qualified audit reports

The auditor will qualify his or her opinion on the financial statements if:

- There is a limitation on the scope of the auditors' examination, or

- The auditors disagree with the treatment or disclosure of a matter in the financial statements,

And, in the auditor's judgement, the effect of the matter is or may be *material* (explained below) to the financial statements which therefore may/do not give a *true and fair view* (explained below) of the matters on which the auditors are required to report or do not comply with relevant accounting or other information.

So if something is wrong with the financial statements, the auditors must say so. Moreover, they are required to give as detailed an explanation as possible, including the quantitative effects on the relevant figures in the financial statements. We will look at qualifications in more detail in Chapter 22.

### True and fair

'True and fair' is a legal term; there is an over-riding requirement in CA 1985 that accounts give a true and fair view.

*S 226 Duty to prepare individual accounts*

- The directors of every company must prepare, for each financial year of the company:
  - Balance sheet as at the last day of the year
  - Profit and loss account

- The balance sheet must give a true and fair view of the state of affairs of the company as at the end of the financial year; and the P&L a/c must give a true and fair view of the profit or loss for the financial year

- A company's accounts must comply with the provisions of Schedule 4 in respect of form and content

- Additional notes may be provided; departure from the Schedule 4 provisions if required for a true and fair view; reasons for departure should be given in the notes to the accounts

*Definition*

CA 1985 does not define true and fair. A literal interpretation might be as follows.

- *True*: information is not false but factual and conforming with reality; in addition the information conforms with required standards and law; in practical terms the accounts have been correctly extracted from the books and records

- *Fair*: information is free from discrimination and bias and in compliance with expected standards and rules; practically, the accounts should reflect the commercial substance of the company's underlying transactions

S 235 states that the audit report must include an opinion on whether such a true and fair view has been given.

The courts will treat compliance with accepted accounting principles as *prima facie* evidence that the accounts are true and fair: confirmed in *Littlejohn v Lloyd Cheynham*

*Ultimately true and fair must be decided by a judge.*

## Materiality

SAS 600 gives the following definition.

- *Material:* a matter is material if its omission or mis-statement would reasonably influence the decisions of a user of the financial statements

- Materiality may be considered in the context of the financial statements as a whole, any individual primary statement within the financial statements or individual items included in them

Note that 'financial statements' are the balance sheet, P&L a/c, statements of cash flows and total recognised gains and losses, notes and other statements and explanatory material, all of which are identified in the auditors' report as being the financial statements.

> *Exam hint.* The contents of this chapter are very important. You should learn the contents of the audit report (although you will not have to produce a whole report in the exam) and *learn* and *understand* the definitions of 'true and fair' and 'materiality'.

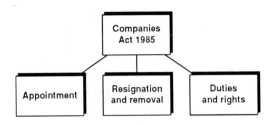

Most audit work is concerned with companies incorporated under the CA 1985, which has been amended in various respects by the CA 1989.

The Companies Act legislation serves a number of purposes.

- It seeks to ensure the competence of auditors by requiring appropriate professional qualifications

- It promotes the independence of the auditor by disqualifying certain persons for appointment as auditor and by means of rules regarding the removal and resignation of the auditor

- It sets out the duties of the auditor

- It gives the auditor certain rights to help him to carry out his duties

The statutory regulations cover three main areas.

- Conduct of an audit and reporting (as covered in Chapters 4 and 21)

- Eligibility and supervision of auditors (Chapter 3)

- Appointment, removal and resignation of auditors

## Appointment

*Annual appointment of auditors: s 385*

- At *each* general meeting of the company at which accounts are laid, *the company* must appoint auditors to hold office until the next general meeting at which accounts are laid

- The *first auditors* of a company may be appointed by *the directors* before the first general meeting and they will hold office until the end of that meeting; or, if the directors fail to do so, they may be appointed by *the company* in general meeting

*Election by private company to dispense with annual appointment: s 386*

- The company may by elective resolution dispense with the obligation to appoint auditors annually

- Auditors are deemed to be reappointed for each succeeding financial year unless a resolution has been passed to terminate the appointment

- Should the election cease the rules of ss 385 and 385A take over

*Casual vacancies: s 388*

The directors or shareholders may appoint auditors to fill a casual vacancy.

*Remuneration of auditors: s 390A*

- Remuneration shall be fixed by the company in general meeting

- State in a note to the accounts the remuneration (including expenses and benefits) of the company's auditors in their capacity as such

**Resignation and removal**

*Resignation: s 392*

- An auditor may resign at any time by sending notice in writing to the company's registered office

- This notice is not effective unless it contains either:
  - o A statement that there are no circumstances connected with his resignation which he considers should be brought to the notice of members or creditors of the company, or
  - o A statement of such circumstances

The company must send a copy of this notice of resignation to the Registrar (< 14 days) and everyone entitled to receive copies of the annual accounts.

*Rights of resigning auditor to requisition company meeting: s 392A*

- Where a statement of circumstances (per above) is included in the resignation notice, the auditor may call on the directors of the company to convene an EGM so that he can explain

- The auditor must request the company to circulate the statement of circumstances connected with his resignation

- The company must notify the members in the notice of meeting that the statement of circumstances has been received, or if requested send the statement out

- Copies of the statement need not be sent out if the court is satisfied the rights are being abused to secure needless publicity for defamatory matter

*Removal of auditors: s 391, s 391A*

- The company can remove the auditor at any time via an Ordinary Resolution, requiring special notice

- Copy of notice is sent to auditor to be removed (and the proposed appointment)

- Auditor has a right to make written representations (circulated) or request that they be read out at the meeting

- Defamatory matter not circulated (as above)

- Auditor has a right to be heard at GM
  - At which term of office would have expired
  - To fill a casual vacancy caused by removal

- The company must send notice of removal to the Registrar within 14 days

*Statement by person ceasing to hold office as auditor: s 394*

- When ceasing to hold office for whatever reason the auditor must deposit at the company's registered office a statement of circumstances to be brought to the attention of members or creditors, or if none state none

- If circumstances are to be notified the company must < 14 days:
  - Send a copy to everyone entitled to the accounts
  - Apply to the court, notifying the auditor

- The auditor waits 21 days, then within a further 7 sends a copy to the Registrar

- The court may direct that the statement need not be sent out; the company has 14 days to notify those entitled to a copy of the accounts of the ruling

## Duties and rights

*Duties*

The main duties of the auditors are contained in ss 235 and 237 CA 1985 and relate to the reporting role of the auditor. The auditor must consider the following provisions.

- Compliance with legislation
- Truth and fairness of accounts
- Proper records and returns
- Agreement of accounts to records
- Consistency of directors' report

S 237 embodies the principle of 'exception reporting'.

*Rights*

Some of the rights of auditors who are removed or who resign are listed above; other rights are as follows.

- Access to records
- Information and explanations
- Attendance at/notices of general meetings
- Right to speak at general meetings
- Rights in relation to written resolutions
- Right to require laying of accounts

*Exam hint.* Do not worry about section numbers - learn the *content* of the legislation.

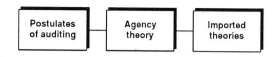

## Postulates of auditing

Auditing theory supports and justifies practice. Postulates of auditing originally laid down by Mautz and Sharaf and subsequently developed.

*Definition*

*Postulate*: something which is assumed to be true as the basis for an argument, something taken for granted. There are no means of directly verifying or proving postulates and they represent 'facts of life' which cannot be further reduced and which must be accepted in order to operate in the field.

If the auditing postulates are not true, then auditing as a discipline has no defence because certain issues cannot be resolved (such as independence).

*Mautz and Sharaf: the eight postulates*

- Financial statements and financial data are verifiable

- There is no necessary conflict of interest between the auditor and the management of the enterprise under audit

- The financial statements and other information submitted for verification are free from collusive and other unusual irregularities

- The existence of a satisfactory system of internal control eliminates the probability of irregularities

- Consistent application of generally accepted accounting principles (GAAP) results in the fair presentation of financial position and the results of operations

- In the absence of clear evidence to the contrary, what has held true in the past for the enterprise under examination will hold true in the future

- When examining financial data for the purpose of expressing an independent opinion thereon, the auditor acts exclusively in the capacity of an auditor

- The professional status of the independent auditor imposes commensurate professional obligations

*Further developments*

The postulates defined above have provided a good basis for auditing theory, leading to new research, theory and practices.

Robertson added a *ninth postulate* which seems of the utmost importance, that audited information is more useful than unaudited information.

It does not state to whom such information is useful but it demonstrates the link between agency theory (see below) and auditing theory.

## Agency theory

The auditor acts as an 'agent' on behalf of the shareholders. Owner-managers take on additional external finance and this will lead to an increased demand for better and more timely and reliable financial information.

The cost of each shareholder individually checking the accounts would be far too high, so 'agency costs' are shared amongst the investors by employing an auditor. This enforces the fiduciary duties of the managers, making them likely to act in the shareholders' interest rather than for their own gain.

## Imported theories

There is a large variety of theories relating to the many different aspects of the auditor's work. These are represented by the variety of tasks the auditor undertakes during the course of a statutory audit relating to:

- Management
- Accounting and finance
- Economics
- Information technology
- Communications

---

*Exam hint.* You are unlikely to be asked a whole question on auditing theory, but you could try to mention the postulates or agency theory when discussing the independence, say, or general role of the auditor.

---

## New audit engagement

There are additional audit considerations when a new audit client is obtained.

*Before accepting nomination*

- Ensure properly qualified to act ie independent, competent

- Ensure firm's resources are adequate to service client's needs ie staff, expertise, time

- Obtain references in respect of new client, eg Dun & Bradstreet, and assess risk

- Communicate with present auditor (if any)

*Communication with present auditor*

Rules of Professional Conduct Statement 5 *Changes in professional appointment*.

- Obtain client's permission to communicate with present auditor

- If refused decline nomination

- Then, write to auditor requesting information which may help decision whether to accept nomination

*Present auditor*

On receiving the above request the present auditor should proceed as follows.

- Request client's permission to discuss affairs freely

- If refused inform proposed new auditor (who should de cline nomination)

- Discuss freely all relevant matters

*After accepting nomination*

- Ensure outgoing auditor's removal/resignation properly conducted in accordance with CA 1985 (as before)

- Ensure new appointment properly conducted

- Send out letter of engagement to directors (see below)

## Engagement letter

The auditing guideline *Engagement letters* covers this area.

*Purpose*

- To define clearly the auditor's responsibilities and minimise possibility of misunderstandings

- Confirms auditor's acceptance of nomination/appointment, scope of audit, form of report

*Procedures*

- Contents discussed with management before sent

- Sent to all new clients

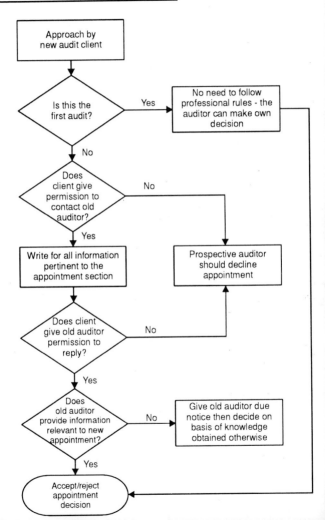

- Once agreed by client, remains effective from one audit appointment to another until replaced

- Review annually to ensure appropriate

- Discuss any changes with management and send revised letter

*Contents and format*

- *Explain statutory responsibilities of client*
  - Maintain proper accounting records
  - Prepare financial statements which give a true and fair view and comply with CA 1985

- *Explain statutory and professional responsibilities of auditor*
  - Report to members on whether in his opinion financial statements give a true and fair view and comply with CA 1985
  - Satisfy himself whether directors' report is consistent with audited financial statements
  - Report if financial statements do not comply in any material respect with SSAPs/FRSs unless he thinks this is justified

- *Explain scope of audit*
  - Conducted in accordance with approved auditing standards and having regard to relevant auditing guidelines
  - Auditor will obtain understanding of accounting system to assess its adequacy as the basis for preparation of financial statements
  - Auditor will seek relevant and reliable evidence, sufficient to enable him to draw reasonable conclusions therefrom

- Nature and extent of tests will vary according to the auditor's assessment of the accounting system, and, where he wishes to rely on it, the system of internal control

- Auditor will report to management any significant weaknesses in, or observations on, the systems

- Indicate that prior to completion of audit written *representations from management* may be sought

- Clarify responsibilities re *irregularities and fraud*
  - Responsibility for prevention and detection
  - Fulfilled by installation of adequate system of internal control
  - Auditor will plan audit so as to have a reasonable expectation of detecting material misstatements in the financial statements resulting from irregularities or fraud

- Adequately describe nature and scope of *services other than audit* to be provided eg accounting and taxation

- Basis of computing, rendering and paying fees

- Request that management confirm in writing their agreement to terms of engagement

---

*Exam hint.* Questions on appointment may be closely connected to ethics - ie is it ethical to accept appointment and if so what are the procedures?

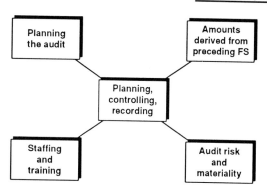

## Planning, controlling, recording

*Auditor's Operational Standard:* to ensure an audit is carried out effectively and efficiently, work needs to be planned, controlled and recorded at each stage regardless of the *size of enterprise.*

*Planning*

- *Form and nature* of planning affected by:
  - Size and complexity of enterprise
  - Commercial environment
  - Method of processing transactions
  - Reporting requirements

- *Benefits of planning*
  - Establishes intended means of achieving the objectives
  - Assists in direction and control of work
  - Helps ensure attention devoted to critical aspects
  - Ensures work is completed expeditiously

- *Procedures*
  - o Review matters raised in last year's audit
  - o Assess effects of changes in legislation, accounting practice
  - o Review interim/management accounts
  - o Consult with management
  - o Identify significant changes in accounting procedures

- *Other considerations*
  - o Timing of significant phases in preparation of financial statements
  - o Extent to which analyses and summaries can be prepared by the entity's employees
  - o Relevance of work done by internal audit
  - o Number, experience, skills of audit staff required
  - o Timing of audit visits

*Controlling*

There are two elements concerned with control.

- Direction and supervision of audit staff
- Review of the work of audit staff

The following objectives should be addressed.

- Work allocated to staff with appropriate training, experience and proficiency

- Audit staff understand responsibilities and objectives

- Working papers adequately record work carried out

- Work performed by audit staff reviewed by more senior persons

Further points for consideration include:

- Audit completion checklists are useful
- Consult another experienced accountant where necessary

*Recording*

- *Reasons for preparing working papers*
  - Satisfy reporting partner that delegated work has been properly performed
  - Future reference
  - Methodical approach

- *Contents*
  - Complete and detailed, so an experienced auditor with no previous connection with the audit can tell from them what work was performed and that the conclusions reached are supported
  - Summary of all significant matters requiring exercise of judgement, with auditor's conclusions thereon
  - Where judgement questioned later, with benefit of hindsight, conclusion based on facts known at the time can be reviewed

- *Ownership and custody*
  - Working papers are property of the auditor
  - Procedures should be adopted to ensure their safe custody and confidentiality

## Planning the audit

- Review existing *engagement letter*

- Review of *client's business* ie overview of industry

- Review of *client's current operations*
  - Accounting system
  - Business locations
  - Organisation chart
  - Internal audit department

- Preliminary *client meeting*
  - Views on current situation
  - Changes
  - Work client staff can do for you
  - Computer access time
  - Last year's management letter follow up

- Prepare detailed *audit approach*
  - Materiality level
  - Critical (risk) areas
  - Audit programmes: P&L a/c, B/S

- Audit *administration*
  - Selection of staff; are specialists required?
  - Time/cost budget
  - Key dates

- Document the above in an *audit planning memorandum:*
  - Terms of engagement
  - Overview of business, financial position, changes
  - Risk areas highlighted, assessment of client's controls
  - Materiality levels
  - Overall audit approach, timing, deadlines, staffing
  - Fees: a detailed time budget is normally attached
  - Signed by audit partner
  - Circulate to audit staff

- Hold a briefing meeting if required

## Amounts derived from preceding FS

The auditor is not required to express an opinion on the corresponding amounts as such, but to ensure that they are the amounts which appeared in the preceding period's financial statements (restated where appropriate).

*Relevance to current period's audit*

- Opening position, eg opening stock has direct impact on current period's profit

- Accounting policies: consistent

- Corresponding amounts: properly disclosed

*Preceding period qualified (and audited by present auditor)*

- Check balances correctly brought forward
- Ensure corresponding amounts properly disclosed

*Preceding period not audited by present auditor*

- Consultations with management

- Review of client's records, working papers, procedures for preceding period

- Audit work on current period

- Consultations with previous auditor (but no legal or ethical obligation for them to cooperate)

- In exceptional circumstances, substantive testing of opening balances

If the auditor is not satisfied, then may have to qualify in respect of the opening position and the consequential effect on the current period.

## Audit risk and materiality

These subjects are closely related and both are of vital importance to the auditor.

*Audit risk (AR)*

- AR = overall risk that the audit opinion is incorrect

- AR is made up of three component parts:
  - *Inherent risk* (IR): the risk that the accounts contain an error
    - Cash businesses
    - Dependence on key products/customers
    - High technology industries
    - Economic environment in that business sector
    - New audit engagements
  - *Control risk* (CR): the risk that the client's system of internal control does not detect the risk
    - Loss of accounts staff/high staff turnover
    - Rapid growth
    - New computer systems, changes to procedures
    - Management override
    - Reporting deadlines unusually soon after year end
  - *Detection risk* (DR): the risk that the type and extent of audit tests carried out do not detect the risk
    - *Non-sampling risk*: incorrect design or performance of tests; incorrect conclusions drawn
    - *Sampling risk*: sample selected not representative of population

- $AR = IR \times CR \times DR$

- At the planning stage the auditor must assess IR and CR and use this to determine the audit work to be carried out

See diagram overleaf.

*Materiality*

What is materiality? We have already discussed this in Chapter 4.

- With the exception of specific disclosure requirements (eg directors' emoluments), company law and accounting standards only apply to material items

- An item can be considered material if its inclusion or misstatement in a set of financial statements could reasonably alter the view of the accounts formed by the reader

- The auditor's 'opinion' as to the truth and fairness of the financial statements lends credibility to them, so the auditor must consider the view given by the accounts to the users

- The auditor must be concerned with identifying 'material' errors, omissions, misstatements, so must set materiality level based on *judgement*

- The level set has a critical impact on the audit in three ways:
  - The nature and size of audit tests
  - Whether to seek adjustments
  - The degree of any audit report qualification

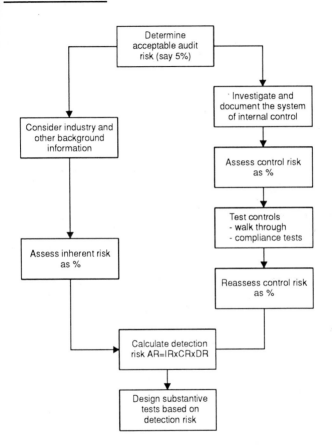

When calculating materiality, the following points should be considered.

- Not a science; no precise figure; matter of professional judgement

- Most firms set criteria for guidance; the manager calculates these and picks an appropriate figure from within the ranges, for example:
  - Between ½% and 1% of turnover
  - Between 1% and 2% of net assets
  - Between 5% and 10% of net profit

- Depends on the auditor's confidence in the client's figures, the uses the financial statements will be put to etc

See diagram overleaf.

## Staffing and training

This is an aspect of controlling the audit which is associated with quality control: see Chapter 24.

### *Continuing professional education (CPE)*

Staff, even when qualified, should be updated technically and given additional training on a regular basis.

CPE has been formalised by the accountancy bodies.

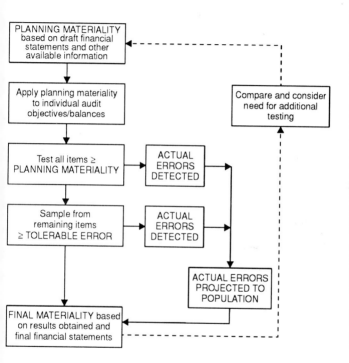

*Reliance on other specialists*

This subject is governed by an auditing guideline. The type of specialists the auditor may wish to rely on will include valuers, architects, actuaries, lawyers, stockbrokers, quantity surveyors.

Audit considerations include:

- Materiality/risk of error
- Complexity of information
- Own knowledge/understanding
- Alternative sources of audit evidence

Requests for specialist evidence should be by the client, or with the client's permission. The auditor has no responsibility to seek evidence independently; audit report qualification if necessary. Before placing reliance on a specialist, the auditor will consider the following.

- *Competence*
  - Technical qualification/membership of professional body
  - Experience
  - Established reputation

- *Objectivity/independence*
  - Relationship between specialist and client
  - Financial interest of specialist in client
  - Professional duties of specialist

- *Agreement on scope of work between auditor, specialist and client*: terms of reference should be documented and confirmed in writing, and should include:
  - Objectives, scope and subject matter of specialist's work
  - Sources of information to be provided to the specialist
  - Assumptions upon which specialist's report depends
  - Form and content of specialist's report

Evaluation of the specialist's findings will involve the following.

- Data provided by specialist is compatible with FS
- Assumptions compatible with FS, consistent with prior years
- Information in accordance with agreement
- Any qualifications in specialist's opinion
- Effective date is acceptable
- Findings fairly reflected in FS

The auditor should obtain a *general understanding* of the assumptions and bases used by the specialist, and consider *whether they appear reasonable*, given his knowledge of the client's business, and consistent with other audit evidence.

The auditor may consider qualifying the audit report in the following circumstances.

- Management unwilling/unable to obtain specialist evidence

- Relevance and reliability of specialist's evidence remains uncertain

- Management refuses to accept and make use of specialist evidence which is relevant, reliable and material to the financial statements

- Management refuses to agree to the appointment of another specialist when the auditor considers that a second opinion is needed

Normally, do not identify specialist in the audit report.

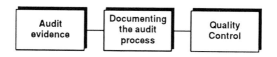

## Audit evidence

Audit evidence is any information obtained by the auditor in arriving at his opinion on the financial statements.

*Sources of evidence*

- Accounting system
- Underlying documentation
- Tangible assets
- Management/employees
- Customers/suppliers/other third parties

The auditor must judge how much and what kind of evidence required, considering:

- Materiality
- Relevance and reliability of evidence available
- Cost and time in obtaining it

There are three elements to the auditor's consideration of audit evidence: sufficiency, relevance and reliability.

*Sufficiency*

The auditor must use judgement in considering what is sufficient to enable him or her to form an opinion, influenced by:

- Knowledge of business
- Risk of misstatement
- Persuasiveness of evidence

*Relevance*

Evidence should enable the auditor to draw reasonable conclusions on the audit objectives.

- *Balance sheet*
  - *Completeness*: have all assets and liabilities been recorded?
  - *Ownership*: are assets/liabilities 'owned' by the enterprise?
  - *Valuation*: have amounts been arrived at in accordance with the stated accounting policies, on an acceptable and consistent basis?
  - *Existence*: do assets and liabilities exists?
  - *Disclosure*: have the assets, liabilities, capital and reserves been properly disclosed?

- *P&L a/c*
  - *Completeness*: have all income and expenses been properly recorded?
  - *Existence*: did the recorded income and expense transactions occur?
  - *Valuation*: have the income and expenses been measured in accordance with the stated accounting policies, on an acceptable and consistent basis?
  - *Disclosure*: have income and expenses been properly disclosed?

*Reliability*

Depends on circumstances, but there are three general presumptions.

- Documentary better than oral

- Independent better than sources within the enterprise

- Evidence originated by auditor via analysis/physical inspection better than originated by others

## Documenting the audit process

The need to *record* the audit process was looked at in Chapter 8. Here we look at the *working papers* themselves.

The exact form of working papers is not prescribed: each firm/individual audit will have its unique characteristics, but what might *typically* be contained in working papers is as follows.

- Information of continuing importance to the audit, eg Memorandum and Articles

- Audit planning information

- Auditor's assessment of the enterprise's accounting system; review and evaluation of its internal controls

- Details of the audit work carried out, notes of errors/exceptions found, action taken thereon, conclusions drawn by the audit staff who performed various sections of the work

- Evidence that the work of the audit staff has been properly reviewed

- Records of relevant balances and other financial information, including analysis and summaries supporting the financial statements

- A summary of significant points affecting the financial statements and the audit report, showing how these points were dealt with

Conventionally there is a division into *current* audit files and *permanent* audit files.

*Permanent file* contents might include the following.

- Legal documents
- Background information
- Organisation charts
- System description
- ICQs
- Letter of engagement
- Correspondence
- Notes of meetings
- Group structure/companies
- Ratio analysis
- Accounting policies etc
- Audit approach
- Matters arising/decisions made

Typical contents of a *current* audit file would be as follows.

- Audited FS, audit report etc
- Audit programme
- Audit planning matters
- Analyses of individual items
- All relevant audit evidence
- Audit conclusions
- Meetings/correspondence
- Detailed audit tests
- Queries and resolutions
- Letter of representation
- PBSE, going concern etc review
- Names, initials of audit staff

All work should be adequately cross-referenced.

## Quality control

We have looked at control of the audit in Chapter 8 and quality control will also be covered in Chapter 24. Here, however, we can concentrate on *review procedures*.

- Throughout the audit, a system of review of all working papers will be used.
  - In the case of a large audit, the work of junior audit staff will be reviewed by the audit senior(s)
  - The audit manager will review the work of the audit senior and at least some of the work of the audit juniors
  - The overall and final review will be undertaken by the partner responsible for the audit opinion

- Each working paper should be initialled (or signed) and dated by the person who prepared it

- When a review takes place, the reviewer will often use a separate working paper to record queries *and* their answer

It is common to have a debriefing meeting at the end of an audit, as a final review stage.

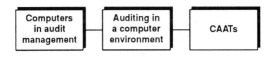

The audit of computer systems is covered in Chapter 26. In this chapter, we look at how computers are used by the auditor as an aid to his or her work and at specific Computer Assisted Audit Techniques (CAATs).

## Computers in audit management

The use of computers in many areas has increased dramatically over the last few years and auditing is no exception. The following are the main computer aids used by auditors.

- *Automated working papers*
  - Calculate ratios/statistics
  - Automatic update of other WPs/TB
  - Neat and tidy
  - Automatic cross-referencing

- *Statistical sampling and analytical review*
  - Information direct from client system
  - Easy to change/manipulate
  - Add to year on year, cumulative
  - Determine sample sizes, generate random numbers etc

- *Decision support systems*
  - Aids to decision-making
  - Checklists eg ICEQs

Controls over audit computers include:

- Security

- Completeness of input, processing and output
- Accuracy of input, processing and output

## Auditing in a computer environment

Before we go on to look at CAATs, a general introduction is required on auditing in a computer environment, to show in particular why CAATs are useful.

The *basic principle* is that the *Auditor's Operational Standard* and audit guidelines apply irrespective of the system of recording and processing transactions.

*Problems* in a computer system are:

- Lack of visible evidence
- Systematic errors
- Loss of 'audit trail'

*Audit approach*

- *Planning*
  - Auditor needs an appropriate level of technical knowledge and skill
  - Decide on effect system will have on timing and manner of performing and recording work
  - Consider use of CAATs

- *Recording systems*
  - Same standard expected of audit working papers as in other areas
  - May require to keep technical papers separate from other working papers; where CAAT used, record:
    - Work performed by CAAT
    - Results of CAAT
    - Auditor's conclusions

- Resolution of technical problems
- Recommendations about any modification of CAAT

- *Controlling work:* where CAATs used, special attention paid to:
  - Co-ordinating work of staff with specialist computer skills
  - Approval and review of technical work by someone with the necessary expertise

- *Evaluate systems*: the auditor will require a detailed record of the system

- *Audit evidence*: CAATs may be used to obtain audit evidence in compliance and substantive testing

- *Review of FS:* CAATs (especially audit software) may be used

## CAATs

Factors affecting use:

- Loss of audit trail
- Cost effectiveness
- Ability to combine tests within CAAT
- Timescale
- Computer facilities
- Frequency of attendance by auditor
- Expertise and experience of audit staff
- Reliance on internal audit

### Types of CAAT

CAATs will be used on the client's own system, so co-operation is required from the client, particularly in terms of computer time and any disruption of normal routine. CAATs are primarily used for compliance testing and are usually suited only to larger assignments.

- *File interrogation*: the performance of transactions within files to ensure controls are operating as specified

- *Test data*: the submission of dummy data to ensure it is processed correctly; can be conducted 'live' or 'dead' ie as part of normal processing or at times when the computer is not in business use

- *Embedded audit facilities* aim to extend the compliance testing more fully throughout the period than test data:
  - SCARF (Systems Control and Review File): taking real transactions at random and replicating their output in a separate file for later investigation
  - ITF (Integrated Test Facilities): gradually releasing test date into live processing and producing exception reports where output differs from that expected; especially useful for clients with strong internal audit

---

*Exam hint*. When devising a CAAT to apply to a question, you must consider the unique characteristics of the situation to which you are applying it - be specific about what the CAAT should do and how it helps the audit.

---

## Internal controls

*Definition*

The auditing guideline *Internal controls* describes the system of internal controls as follows.

> 'The whole system of controls, financial and otherwise, established by the management in order to carry on the business of the enterprise in an orderly and efficient manner, ensure adherence to management policies, safeguard the assets and secure as far as possible the completeness and accuracy of the records.'

*Importance to the auditor*

- Management responsibility to set up a system of controls appropriate to the enterprise

- Auditor will ascertain, evaluate and perform compliance tests on their operation

- If the auditor obtains reasonable assurance via compliance tests that controls are effective in ensuring the completeness and accuracy of accounting records, and validity of entries therein, the extent of substantive testing may be limited

## Types of internal control

Segregation of duties
Organisation
Authorisation and approval
Physical
Supervisory
Personnel
Arithmetic and accounting
Management

---

*Exam hint.* Whenever you are asked to comment on internal controls, or suggest appropriate internal controls, write the above list out first. Jot down the relevant controls *appropriate to the system in the question* under each one to produce an answer.

---

## Ascertaining/evaluating the system

*The accounting system*

The auditing guideline *Accounting systems* covers this area.

- The auditor will review the accounting system and records:
  - To determine nature of audit tests
  - To discharge his responsibility under s 237 CA 1985 to form an opinion on the adequacy of the accounting records

- Management require complete and accurate accounting records:
  - To control the business
  - To safeguard the assets
  - To prepare financial statements
  - To comply with legislation: s 221(1) CA 1985

- The accounting records contain:
  - Entries from day to day of all sums of money received and expended by the company
  - The matters in respect of which the receipt and expenditure takes place
  - A record of the assets and liabilities of the company

- Depending on the size and nature of the business, an accounting system will often incorporate internal controls to ensure that:
  - All transactions have been recorded
  - Errors or irregularities in processing will become apparent
  - Assets and liabilities recorded do exist and are recorded at correct amounts

- Extent to which accounting system is recorded and method used will depend on:
  - Complexity and nature of the system
  - Degree of reliance to be placed on internal controls

*Documenting the system*

There are three methods commonly used to document the client's system. Typically, these are performed for new clients or for clients who have installed new systems. They will then be filed in the client's permanent file and updated as necessary each year.

- *Narrative notes*: written, or *word-processed* description of the system:
  - *Advantages*
    - Quick to prepare
    - Sufficient for small or simple systems

- o *Disadvantages*
  - – Difficult to update if handwritten
  - – Difficult to digest if complex system

- *Flowcharts:* diagrammatic representations of the system, usually broken down into separate activities:
  - o *Advantages*
    - – Easier to interpret for larger, more complex systems
    - – Highlight any areas where controls are missing
  - o *Disadvantages*
    - – Time-consuming to prepare
    - – Require understanding of standard symbols

- *Checklists or questionnaires*: audit firm will have a standard list of controls; the audit staff can quickly ascertain which, if any, are in operation at the client:
  - o *Advantages*
    - – Comprehensive list ensures all controls considered
    - – Quick to prepare
    - – Easy to record and control
  - o *Disadvantages*
    - – Client may be able to overstate controls
    - – May contain large number of irrelevant controls
    - – Effective but novel controls are missed

This last method is the means by which *internal controls*, rather than the accounting system, are ascertained. There are two main types of checklist, which fulfil different purposes.

- *Internal Control Questionnaires (ICQs)* are used to discover whether controls exist which meet specified control objectives

- *Internal Control Evaluation Questionnaires (ICEQs)* are used to determine whether these controls prevent or detect *particular* specified errors or omissions

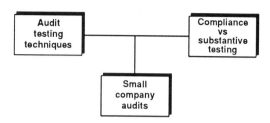

## Audit testing techniques

Audit evidence can be divided into types on the basis of the way in which it is obtained.

- *Inspection* of records and assets: reliable evidence of existence but not ownership

- *Observation* of operating procedures: only provides evidence at the time of performance

- *Enquiry* of knowledgeable persons, in writing, or orally: reliability depends on competence, experience, independence and integrity of respondent

- *Computation*

- *Analytical review* (see Chapter 21)
  - Study significant ratios and trends and investigate any unusual or unexpected variations
  - Review over time, against industry norms, competitors etc
  - Obtain explanations for unexpected variations or lack of variations which were expected
  - Verify explanations or extend detailed testing in these areas

## Compliance vs substantive testing

These are the two types of test which can be used to obtain audit evidence.

*Compliance tests*

Those tests which seek to provide audit evidence that internal control procedures are being applied as prescribed

*Substantive tests*

Those tests of transactions and balances, and other procedures such as analytical review, which seek to provide audit evidence as to the completeness, accuracy and validity of the information contained in the accounting records or in the financial statements.

*Designing tests*

Audit objectives can be related to five attributes.

Completeness
Ownership
Valuation
Existence
Disclosure

The technique used to test the first four of these attributes is referred to as 'directional testing'. (The fifth attribute, disclosure, is tested as part of the review of financial statements.)

- *Debit items* (expenditure/assets): tested for overstatement
- *Credit items* (income/liabilities): tested for understatement

The matrix set out below demonstrates how directional testing is applied to give assurance on all account areas in the financial statements.

| Type of account | Purpose of primary test | Primary test also gives comfort on | | | |
|---|---|---|---|---|---|
| | | Assets | Lia-bilities | Income | Ex-penses |
| Assets | Overstatement (O) | U | O | O | U |
| Liabilities | Understatement (U) | U | O | O | U |
| Income | Understatement (U) | U | O | O | U |
| Expense | Overstatement (O) | U | O | O | U |

Performing the primary tests shown, the auditor obtains assurance in other audit areas; cost-effective.

## Small company audits

The purpose of an audit is to reassure the shareholders that the financial statements prepared by the directors are true and fair. In many small companies, these two parties are the same people.

*Relaxation of the audit requirement*

The response to this has been to relax the regulations regarding what companies require to be audited. Originally proposed by Kenneth Clarke in November 1993 budget:

• Turnover less than £90,000: no audit

• Turnover between £90,000 and £350,000: a 'compilation report' rather than an audit

The ASB's wording for a compilation report (unqualified) is as follows.

ACCOUNTANT'S REPORT TO THE SHAREHOLDERS OF XYZ LIMITED

I have examined without carrying out an audit, the accounts for the year ended ... set out on pages... to....

*Respective    responsibilities    of    directors    and    reporting
accountant*

As described on page... the company's directors are
responsible for the preparation of the accounts, and they
believe that the company is exempt from an audit. It is my
responsibility to examine the accounts and, based on my
examination, to report my opinion, as set out below, to the
shareholders.

*Basis of opinion*

I conducted my examination in accordance with the appropriate
standards for reporting accountants issue by the Auditing
Practices Board. This examination consisted of comparing the
accounts with the accounting records kept by the company,
and making such limited enquiries of the officers of the
company as I considered necessary for the purposes of this
report.

The examination was not an audit conducted in accordance
with auditing standards. Accordingly I do not express an audit
opinion on the accounts. Therefore my examination does not
provide any assurance that the accounting records and the
accounts are free from material misstatement.

*Opinion*

In my opinion:

(a)    the accounts are in agreement with those accounting
       records kept by the company under section 221 of the
       Companies Act 1985;

(b)    having regard only to, and on the basis of, the information
       contained in those accounting records, the accounts have
       been drawn up in a manner consistent with the accounting
       requirements specified in section 249C(4) of the Act; and

(c)  the company satisfied the conditions for exemption from an audit of the accounts for the year specified in section 249A(4) of the Act and did not, at any time within that year, fall within any of the categories of companies not entitled to the exemption specified in the section 249B(1)

*Reporting accountants*                                      *Address*
*Date*

*Considerations for retaining the annual audit*

*Retain audit*                              *Abolish audit*

- The audit, via reports to management, provides useful commercial advice, ie improvement to control/efficiency

- For most small firms the auditor will also act as accountant/tax adviser and the relative costs of removing audit work will be low

- If companies wish to save the audit fee they can become partnerships/sole traders

- Compilation report will not be any cheaper

- The regulatory regime of the RSBs provides quality control safeguards which will be lost as reporting accountant need not be Registered Auditor

- It is an unfair burden on companies

- If 'other users' wish to rely on the financial statements they can require an audit to be conducted (and hence greater opportunity for 'auditor' to be liable)

- Other users do not rely on audit report (hence credit rating agencies, PAYE and VAT inspections)

- If companies wanted an audit report included with their accounts, they could still have one

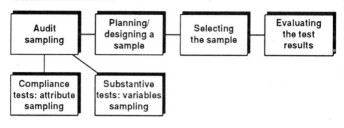

## Audit sampling

*Definition*

The application of audit procedures to less than 100% of the items within an account balance or class of transactions in order to assist in forming a conclusion concerning that account balance or class of transactions.

*Why sample?*

It is not cost-effective for the auditor to test every item appearing in the financial statements.

- For some items, eg movements in directors' loan accounts, a 100% check may be performed but this is a high risk area and it not likely to contain many transactions

- In most cases, eg stock, debtors or sales, there is too great a volume of transactions for this 100% check to be cost-effective

Therefore, the auditor must gain sufficient assurance that the total amount stated in the accounts is correct by sampling, testing only a proportion of the items which comprise the total.

Stages of the sampling process are:

1   Planning/designing the sample
2   Selecting the items to be tested

3    Testing the items (using methods described elsewhere)
4    Evaluating the results of the tests

Items 1, 2, and 4 concern us here.

## Planning/designing a sample

When designing an audit sample, the auditors should consider the specific *audit objectives*, the *population* from which they wish to sample and the *sample size* (SAS 430.2).

- *Audit objectives*: the nature and purpose of the test must be clearly identified:
  - Is it a *compliance test*, did a control operate properly?
  - Is it a substantive test, more concerned with monetary value?

- *Population:* this is the entire set of data from which the auditor will select the sample; the auditor must also consider his audit objectives here, so ensuring for instance that in testing for overstatement the population would be drawn from the financial statements

- When determining the *sample size* the auditor would consider *sampling risk*, the *tolerable error* and the *expected error* (SAS 430.3)

*Sampling risk*

Ignoring inherent risk for now: AR = CR × DR

If we accept, as our firm's policy, audit risk = 2% for all circumstances, then the degree of assurance we require from our substantive tests will be determined by the control risk (that risk where the client has failed to detect and correct errors). If we feel that the client's system of control is poor then we will require more confidence in our substantive tests.

- If CR = 50%, DR = 4%, ie 96% confidence that the population is representative

- If CR = 25%, DR = 8%, ie 92% confidence that the population is representative

The assessment of control risk is important; if it is set too high we will over-audit. If we overestimate the effectiveness of the control system, ie we set CR too low, then we will under-audit.

Audit risk is set by audit firms as an internal policy.

*Tolerable error*

Tolerable error is the maximum error or error rate in the population which the auditor can accept and still conclude that the audit objective has been achieved.

- For substantive tests the tolerable error is set based on materiality

- For compliance tests the tolerable error is the maximum number of times a control has not operated properly whilst allowing the auditor to conclude no material misstatements occurred

- The smaller the tolerable error, the large the sample size needs to be

*Expected error*

Where a population is expected to be error free, a smaller sample can be justified. Expected errors are set by assessing control risk (either setting it informally or setting it to a specific item in the financial statements).

## Selecting the sample

The auditor should select sample items in such a way that the sample can be expected to be *representative* of the population (SAS 430.4), ie all items in the population have an opportunity of being selected.

While there are a number of selection methods, three methods commonly used are as follows.

- *Random selection*: ensures that all items in the population have an equal chance of selection, eg by use of random number tables

- *Systematic selection*: selecting items using a constant interval between selections, the first interval having a random start; ensure that the population is not structured in such a manner that the sampling interval corresponds with a particular pattern in the population

- *Haphazard selection*; may be an acceptable alternative to random selection provided the auditors are satisfied that the sample is not unrepresentative of the entire population: care needs to be taken to guard against making a selection which is biased, eg towards items which are easily located

## Evaluating the test results

(SAS 430.5): having carried out, on each sample item, those audit procedures which are appropriate to the particular audit objective, the auditors should:

- Analyse any errors detected in the sample
- Project the errors found in the sample to the population
- Reassess the sampling risk

*Analysis of errors in the sample*

- What is the nature and cause of the error?

- Is there a possible effect on other areas of the audit?
- Is it a genuine error?

*Reassessment of sampling risk*

The auditors need to consider whether errors in the population might exceed the tolerable error.

- Compare the *projected population* error to tolerable error, taking account of other related audit results
- If projected error > tolerable error, reassess sampling risk
- If sampling risk now unacceptable, extend audit procedure or perform alternative procedure(s)
- Adjustment to financial statements may be required on this basis

## Compliance tests: attribute sampling

Testing to see if a control has operated irrespective of the value of the transaction itself ie monetary values are irrelevant.

- *Attribute sampling* is to test for a specific characteristic of the item selected: in a compliance test Yes or No, the control did or did not operate
- *Sample selection* would be on a systematic basis normally
- Care must be taken that the population does not have a regular pattern

## Substantive tests: variables sampling

*Variables sampling* is concerned with sampling units which can take a value within a continuous range of possible values and is used to provide conclusions as to the monetary value of a population. The auditor can use it to estimate the value of a population by extrapolating statistically the value of a representative sample of items drawn from the population.

*Monetary Unit Sampling (MUS)*

MUS produces conclusions based on monetary amounts, *not* occurrence rates, by defining each £1 of a population as a separate sampling unit.

Sample size = $\dfrac{\text{Reliability factor} \times \text{Population value}}{\text{Tolerable error}}$

Sampling interval = $\dfrac{\text{Population value}}{\text{Sample size}}$

      *or*   $\dfrac{\text{Tolerable error}}{\text{Reliability factor}}$

The first 'item', or £1, is selected at random.

Points to note include the following.

- By starting at a random point, the items selected are unpredictable

- All values have the opportunity to be selected

- MUS favours higher value transactions

- By setting a minimum permissible R-factor of 1, all material balances will be selected

- The population must be readily converted to give cumulative balances - CAATs can be very useful

- Not all populations have a monetary value eg unpriced sales orders

*Stratification*

If it is appropriate to stratify the population, this may lead to a smaller sample size.

- Allows auditor to focus on high value items
- Selection within strata on random basis
- Time consuming to collate population (CAATs useful)

---

*Exam hint.* No calculations will be required in the exam, other than the most basic type. You are more likely to be asked to *describe* sampling, both in general and in relation to a specific situation: make sure the sampling methods and procedures you describe are *appropriate*.

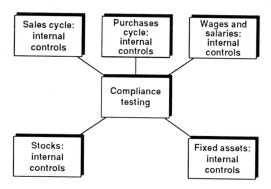

The auditor will have recorded the internal control system whilst recording the accounting system. This will have been a preliminary evaluation, often based on questionnaires.

- If this suggests controls are good, and if the auditor wishes to rely on them, design and perform compliance tests (a cost-effective approach)

- If preliminary evaluation suggests controls are poor, move directly to designing and performing substantive tests and report to management

## Compliance testing

This means testing that the control has operated as it should. The following procedures should be followed.

- Exceptions should be recorded and investigated regardless of amount involved

- Assess whether exceptions are isolated departures or indicate existence of errors in accounting records

- If results unsatisfactory move on to substantive tests and report to management

- When choosing a sample the aim is to spread it throughout the whole period under review

---

*Exam hint.* The examination could include a question on either expected controls, or the compliance tests you would perform *in a particular business*. To answer most effectively, memorise the objectives of the control - these do not vary significantly from business to business - and then apply sensible controls to meet that objective *in the situation given in the question*.

---

## Sales cycle: internal controls

*Authorisation of sales*

- Objectives
  - Completeness of income: ensure all sales made are recorded
  - Safeguard assets: do not sell to bad credit risk
  - Ensure best prices achieved

- Controls
  - Credit customers authorised, especially with reference to credit limits granted
  - Orders accepted by/authorised by responsible officer
  - Ensure production orders/requisitions raised for all orders
  - Controls over outstanding orders
  - Authorisation of trade discounts
  - Properly updated prices quoted to customers
  - Segregate duties between order clerk and authorisation procedure

- Internal Control Evaluation Questionnaires (ICEQs)
  - Can goods be sold to a bad credit risk?

- o   Can sales be missed?
- o   Are all sales properly supported?

*Custody*

- **Objectives**
  - o   Safeguard stock holdings
  - o   Despatch goods only to correct, properly authorised customers

- **Controls**
  - o   Follow-up procedures where stock not available
  - o   Goods despatched only on receipt of authorised sales order
  - o   Despatch note raised
  - o   Checks on quality, quantity and condition of goods despatched
  - o   Customer signs delivery note/sheet as evidence of receipt

- **ICEQs**
  - o   Can goods be despatched but not invoiced?
  - o   Can sales be missed?

*Accounting*

- **Objectives**
  - o   Sundry sales are controlled
  - o   Invoicing errors cannot occur
  - o   All sales are properly supported
  - o   Accounts do not remain overdue
  - o   Safeguarding assets: ensure all credit entries to debtor accounts are controlled

- o Accounts are correctly updated
- o All sales are recognised

- *Controls*
  - o Sales invoice raised for all despatches
  - o Details checked (price, discounts, quantities), evidence of check
  - o Year end procedures for goods despatched uninvoiced
  - o Customer accounts in sales ledger updated, promptly and correctly
  - o Customer statements regularly sent out
  - o Procedure for dealing with customer queries
  - o Procedure for following up overdue accounts
  - o Authorisation of bad debt write-offs
  - o Segregate duties between those updating accounts and reviewing the sales ledger
  - o Numerical sequence used for all sales
  - o All credit notes must be authorised and matched to stock movements

- *ICEQs*
  - o Can invoices be raised but omitted from the records?
  - o Can invoicing errors occur?
  - o Can debtor accounts be improperly credited?
  - o Can debtors be overstated or understated due to year end cut off errors?
  - o Can debts go unchased?
  - o Are cash sales properly dealt with?
  - o Can sales be missed?

*Payments received from customers*

- *Objectives*
  - o Cash is safeguarded
  - o Debtors are promptly and correctly updated so ensuring control over debtor recoveries

- *Controls*
  - o Mail opening procedures (2 persons, add lists, restrictive crossing of cheques)
  - o Segregation of duties between those with custody of cash and update of sales ledger
  - o Daily banking procedures
  - o Sales ledger update checks and routines

- *ICEQs*
  - o Can cash be received and not banked?
  - o Can accounts be improperly credited?

*Reconciliations*

- *Objectives*
  - o To ensure complete and accurate financial statements are prepared
  - o Up-to-date management information available

- *Controls*
  - o Sales ledger control account reconciliations
  - o Management review
  - o Trial balance
  - o Bank reconciliations

- *ICEQ*: are the financial statements complete, accurate and valid?

## Purchases cycle: internal controls

*Authorisation*

- *Objectives*
  - Completeness of expenses and ensure all purchases made are recorded
  - Only purchase quantity and quality required
  - Ensure best prices are achieved

- *Controls*
  - Purchase orders properly authorised before being placed
    - within limits
    - control over blank order and requisition forms
  - Central buying policy
  - Control over unfilled orders

- *ICEQs*
  - Can purchases be missed?
  - Are all purchases properly supported?

*Custody*

- *Objectives*
  - Safeguard stock/other asset holdings
  - To ensure receipt of goods which have been ordered and are undamaged

- *Controls*
  - Goods inward checked on arrival: quantity, quality, condition
  - Check details to purchase order
  - All checks evidenced

   o   Goods received note raised

- *ICEQs*
  - o  Can goods be accepted that have not been ordered?
  - o  Can goods be received and no liability recognised?
  - o  Can goods be received and diverted for private use?
  - o  Can liabilities be generated for faulty goods or short deliveries?

*Accounting*

- *Objectives*
  - o  Sundry purchases are controlled
  - o  Errors in recognition of liability cannot occur
  - o  All purchases are properly supported by relevant documentation
  - o  Safeguarding assets
    - –  Any worthwhile discounts available are taken up
    - –  Any credit notes required are followed up
    - –  Liabilities are not recorded before the receipt of goods or services
  - o  Accounts are correctly updated
  - o  All purchases are recognised

- *Controls*
  - o  Supplier invoice checked to order/GRN: quantity, type, prices
  - o  Creditors ledger updated promptly and checks on accuracy of input
  - o  Procedure for checking suppliers' statements to creditors ledger
  - o  Procedure for accruing uninvoiced GRNs at year end

o Grid stamp completed; accuracy of invoice and posting

- *ICEQs*
  - o Are liabilities only recognised on receipt of authorised goods and for the correct amount?
  - o Can purchases be missed?
  - o Can possible credit note/discount be missed?
  - o Can creditors be overstated or understated due to year end cut off errors?
  - o Are cash purchases properly dealt with?

*Payments*

- *Objectives*
  - o Cash is safeguarded: not paid out to non-supplier
  - o Creditors' accounts are promptly and correctly updated so there is no risk of double payment, or missing out on worthwhile settlement discounts

- *Controls*
  - o Properly authorised by responsible official, cheques raised by cashier
  - o Paid invoices cancelled
  - o Purchase/creditors ledger updated promptly and accuracy tests on posting
  - o Monthly reconciliation of supplier's account balance to supplier statements

- *ICEQs*
  - o Can accounts be improperly debited or not debited on payment?
  - o Can payments be diverted to a non-supplier of goods/services?

- o Can payment be made twice to the same supplier on the same invoice?
- o Is the balance at the bank and petty cash properly recorded at all times?
- o Can unauthorised cash payments be made?

*Reconciliation*

- **Objectives**
  - o To ensure complete and accurate financial statements are prepared
  - o Up-to-date management information available
- **Controls**
  - o Purchase ledger to purchase ledger control account in nominal ledger
  - o Trial balance
- **ICEQs**
  - o Are the financial statements complete, accurate, valid?
  - o Do internal controls operate as intended?

## Wages and salaries: internal controls

*Controls*

- Pay sheets prepared by responsible person
- Authorisation of appointment/discharge of employees
- Authorisation of rates of pay, including charges
- Proper recording of hours worked/work done eg timesheets and review by responsible official
- Overtime properly authorised

- Proper procedures for non-routine circumstances eg absences, advances of pay

- Authorisation of deductions from gross pay

- Payment of cash
  - Procedures to ensure wages cheque cashed is for total of net wages
  - Security over monies during collection, transit and distribution
  - Procedures to verify employee's identity
  - Payment by person independent of preparation of paysheets/packets
  - Controls over unclaimed wages

- Payment by cheque/bank transfers
  - Cheque signatories independent of payroll preparation
  - Cheque signatory reviews payroll

- Employee records held independent of wages and salaries dept

- Review of actual pay against budgets, other periods and investigation of variances

*ICEQs*

Is there reasonable assurance that:

- Employees are only paid for work done?
- Employees are paid the correct amount: gross/net?
- The right employees actually receive the right amount?
- Accounting for payroll costs and deductions is accurate?

## Fixed assets: internal controls

*Controls*

- Authorisation of capital expenditure is evidenced

- Authorisation of sale/transfer/scrapping of fixed assets is evidenced

- Procedures to ensure accounting system distinguishes capital and revenue expenditure

- Fixed asset register maintained and periodically reconciled to nominal ledger accounts

- Regular physical checks on assets

- Authorisation of depreciation rates

*ICEQs*

Is there reasonable assurance that:

- Recorded assets actually exist and belong to the company?
- Capital expenditure is authorised and reported?
- Disposals of fixed assets are authorised and reported?
- Depreciation is realistic?
- Fixed assets are correctly accounted for?

## Stocks: internal controls

*Controls*

- Arrangements for receiving, checking and recording goods inward

- Physical security over stocks: theft, misuse, deterioration

- Independent stock records maintained by responsible person, and periodically reconciled to financial accounts

- Controls over stocks held by others

- Regular physical checks on stocks

- Periodic review for damaged, slow moving and obsolete stocks, with authorisation of stock write offs

*ICEQs*

- Stock safeguarded from physical loss; fire, theft, etc?
- Stock records are accurate and up to date?
- The recorded stock exists?
- The cut off is reliable?
- The costing system is reliable?
- The stock sheets are accurately compiled?
- The stock valuation is fair?

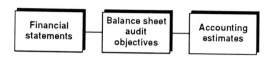

## Financial statements

*Contents*

- *Primary statements*
  - Balance sheet
  - P&L a/c
  - Statement of recognised gains and losses
  - Cash flow statement

- *Notes to the accounts*, including a note of HC profits and losses and the FRS 1 notes to the cash flow statement

- *Directors' report*: contents governed by statute to a certain extent

- *Chairman's report*: a 'blurb'

- *Auditor's report* on the truth and fairness of the accounts

*Assertions*

- SSAP 2 fundamental accounting concepts:
  - Matching
  - Going concern
  - Prudence
  - Consistency

- True and fair: no precise definition

- Fundamental balance sheet assertions
  - Cost
  - Authority
  - Value
  - Existence
  - Beneficial ownership

- Presentation: CA 1985 and SSAPs/FRSs

## Balance sheet audit objectives

Completeness
Ownership
Valuation
Existence
Disclosure

- *Completeness:* all transactions recorded/look for what could be missing

- *Ownership:* assets and liabilities rightly belong to client

- *Valuation:* assets and liabilities shown at correct amounts

- *Existence:* assets and liabilities are real

- *Disclosure:* accounts show true and fair view and all required disclosures made

> *Exam hint.* When tackling a question on the audit of a balance sheet item, jot down the objectives listed above as the starting point in your answer plan.

## Accounting estimates

An approximation of the amount of an item in the absence of a precise means of measurement. Management responsibility; but high risk for the auditor.

*Examples*

- Stock obsolescence/bad debt provisions
- Depreciation provision
- Provision for deferred taxation
- Provision for a loss from a lawsuit
- Profits or losses on construction contracts in progress
- Provision to meet warranty claims

*Audit objectives and procedures*

- Obtain audit evidence regarding *material* accounting estimates

- Obtain audit evidence as to whether an accounting estimate is *reasonable* and appropriately *disclosed*

- Adopt one or a combination of the following approaches:
  - Review and test the process used by management to develop the estimate
  - Use an independent estimate for comparison
  - Review subsequent events to confirm the estimate

- Make a final assessment of the reasonableness of the accounting estimate

In many audits, stock represents one of the riskiest areas for an auditor, being of *high value*, *outside* the normal accounting system and *subjective* as to valuation.

The audit approach must cover the three areas shown above.

**Quantity**

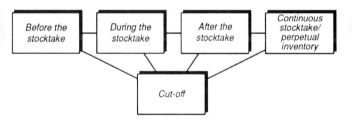

There are three methods whereby the client reaches a final figure for stock.

- Year end count
- Interim count, rolled on to year end
- Continuous stock records and perpetual inventory

A particular technique to verify quantity of stocks is for the auditor to attend the client stocktaking and the relevant procedures are contained in the auditing guideline *Attendance at stocktaking*.

*Before the stocktake*

- *Planning*
    - Review working papers for previous year
    - Determine arrangements with management in advance
    - Become familiar with nature of stocks
    - Stocks held by/for 3rd parties

- Review client's stocktake instructions (part of planning)
    - In writing
    - 2 independent counts
    - Systematic clearing of areas
    - Identification of obsolete/damaged stock
    - Supervision
    - Cut-off
    - Count sheets: prenumbered/ink/controlled
    - Investigation of differences

- Determine audit procedures to cover a representative selection of stocks

- Potential problem/risk areas

*During the stocktake*

- Review client staff
- Test counts: records to goods; goods to records: errors?
- Review for damaged, old, obsolete stocks
- Review WIP for stage of completion
- Ensure stocks held for 3rd parties excluded from count
- Cut-off details
- Overall impression of stock levels/values

*After the stocktake*

- Check sequence of stock sheets
- Check client's computation of final (unit) figure
- Trace own test count items through
- Check replies from 3rd parties
- Inform management of general problems
- Follow up cut-off details
- Ensure necessary adjustments to book stocks made

*Continuous stocktake/perpetual inventory*

- Review company's procedures:
  - Independence of counters
  - Frequency of counts
  - Ensure all lines covered at least once per year
  - Investigation of discrepancies
  - Updating of records

- Attend at least one of the company's counts (to observe)

- Review whole year's results:
  - Extent of counting
  - Accuracy of records

- Do own count at year end:
  - Check to underlying records
  - Review results against company

*Cut-off*

Cut-off is important as it affects which transactions are recorded in which period, so determining when profits are recognised.

Cut-off is most critical to the accurate recording of transactions in a manufacturing enterprise at particular point in the accounting cycle as follows.

- Point of purchase and receipt of goods and services
- Requisitioning of raw materials for production
- Transfer of completed WIP to finished goods stock
- Sale and despatch of finished goods

Audit procedures at the *stocktake* should include the following.

- Record all movement notes relating to the period, including:
  - All interdepartmental requisition numbers
  - The last GRNs and despatch notes prior to the count
  - The first GRNs and despatch notes after the count

- Observe whether correct cut-off procedures are being followed in the despatch and receiving areas and that they are understood by the company staff performing the count

- Ensure that no goods finished on the day of the count are transferred to the warehouse

Procedures during the *final audit* will include the following.

- Match up the GRNs with purchase invoices (or stock accruals where goods had not been invoiced at the year end) and ensure liability recorded in the correct period: only goods received before the year end should be recorded as purchases

- Match up the goods despatched note to sales invoices and ensure the income has been recorded in the correct period: only stocks despatched before the year end should be recorded as sales

- Match up the requisition notes to the WIP figures for the receiving department to ensure correctly recorded

## Valuation

Stocks should be valued at the lower of cost and net realisable value (SSAP 9).

- Record basis of valuation used

- Test material costs:
  - Check to individual invoices
  - Ensure FIFO or appropriate bases being used
  - Check quantities used in WIP/FG

- Test labour costs:
  - Check calculations to supporting documentation
  - Review costing against actual labour

- Test application of overheads:
  - Ensure only production overheads included
  - Ensure based on normal activity levels

- Review stage of completion of WIP:
  - Carry forward count details
  - Reasonable?
  - Calculations

- Net realisable value:
  - Follow through items noted at count
  - Review sales after B/S date
  - Future order book
  - Background knowledge
  - Write-downs last year

## Disclosure

- Accounting policies used in calculating:
  - Cost
  - Net realisable value
  - Attributable profit
  - Foreseeable losses

- Stocks and WIP should be sub-classified as:
  - Raw materials and consumables
  - Work in progress
  - Finished goods
  - Payments on account

*Exam hint.* In every sitting of this exam there will almost certainly be at least one question on the audit of stocks; the examiner sees this as a central part of most audits. If you feel it is necessary, go back to your Paper 1 material and revise SSAP 9 in detail.

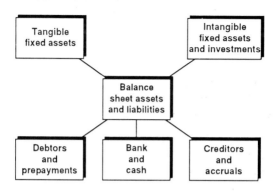

## Tangible fixed assets

The objectives of the fixed asset audit are given here, along with some example tests.

*Completeness*

- Obtain the fixed asset register and reconcile to financial statements

- Test from physical assets to the register

*Ownership*

- For additions inspect purchase invoices, architects' certificates or contracts

- For buildings inspect title deeds, land registry certificates or leases

- For vehicle, check insurance paid

*Valuation*

- Review depreciation rates used considering asset's lives, consistency with prior years and any possible obsolescence

- For revaluations check to supporting documentation of valuer

- Review treatment of capital grants and ensure in accordance with SSAP 4

- Review insurance cover

- Review own work capitalised, particularly costing calculations

*Existence*

- Physically verify assets listed on register
- Review treatment of disposal of fixed assets

*Disclosure*

- Ensure summary of fixed assets is properly disclosed in the financial statements

- Ensure accounting policy note given and correct

## Intangible fixed assets and investments

The main categories of intangible fixed assets are goodwill and development costs. The following substantive procedures are relevant.

*Completeness*

- Obtain schedule of acquisitions and check related goodwill recorded

- Ensure development costs recorded for all R & D projects

*Ownership*

- Check patents, etc registered in the company's name
- Check contracts for purchase of companies
- Check share certificates etc in company's name

*Valuation*

- Check calculations of purchased goodwill
- Check R & D costs to supporting documents
- Check purchase price of patents etc
- Check SSAP 13 capitalisation criteria
- Check amortisation/write-downs: sufficiency etc

*Existence*

- Check share certificates
- Physically verify R & D fixed assets

*Disclosure*

- Ensure full disclosure made in accounts/notes
- Check accounting policy note

## Debtors and prepayments

*Debtors circularisation*

This is a specific technique used to check for the existence and ownership of debtors. Note that it does *not* confirm valuation (ie collectibility). The procedures are as follows.

- Obtain listing of trade debtors as at the year end/confirmation date

- Agree total to sales ledger control (SLC) account (test cast)

- Review for any obvious omissions/misstatements

- Select a sample of accounts for positive confirmation; consider:
  - Old, unpaid amounts
  - Credit balances
  - Nil balances
  - Material balances

- Letter should be on client's paper, signed by client with a copy of the current statement attached; it should request the reply be sent direct to the auditor and reply paid envelopes should be sent

- After reasonable period, send 'follow-up' request

- Telex/phone/fax

- Investigate disputed balances

- If no reply, could try confirmation of individual outstanding invoices or alternative procedures:
  - Agree opening balance on a/c with last year's closing balance
  - Test casts
  - Verify o/s items to back up documentation
  - Review cash received after year end
  - Discuss with responsible company official

The follow-up work required for an *interim circularisation* is as follows.

- Review entries on SLC account for intervening period

- Select sales entries and verify to SDB, sales invoices and despatch notes

- Select GRNs: ensure credit entries posted through to SLC account

- Select cash receipts from cash receipts records: ensure posted to SLC account

- Review list of balances at the circularisation date and at year end: investigate any unexpected differences

- Analytical review at year end

- Cut-off work at year end

*Other tests on debtors*

- *Completeness/existence* (cut-off work)
  - Check goods outwards/returns inward notes around the year end to ensure:
    - Invoices/credit notes dated in correct period
    - Posted to NL/SL in correct period
  - Review receipts from debtors recorded after the year end to ensure these should not have been recorded before year end
  - Review SLC account around the year end for any unusual items
  - Review material post-year end invoices to ensure these are properly treated as next year's sales

- *Valuation*
  - Obtain listing of overdue debts: check the extraction
  - Discuss significant overdue debts with responsible company official
  - Review correspondence to assess recoverability
  - Ensure all debts written off were properly authorised

- *Disclosure*: ensure debtors appropriately categorised within current assets

- *Review debtors analytically*
  - o Ratios
    - – Days sales outstanding
    - – Debtors as % of sales
  - o Compare with previous years/budgets
  - o Obtain and corroborate explanations

## Bank and cash

The main objectives, with example tests, are given below.

*Completeness*

- Review bank confirmation letter for details of all accounts held

- Count petty cash balance

- Check casts of bank reconciliations

- Trace outstanding items to after y/e bank statements and ensure all subsequently cleared

- Review cash book for unusual items

*Ownership*

Review bank letter to ensure valid title to accounts held.

*Existence*

Trace recorded assets and liabilities to bank confirmation of balances.

*Bank letters*

The auditing guideline *Bank report for audit purposes* covers this area. The information which auditors regularly need from banks is substantially the same for most audits, and can be obtained in a standard letter of request. The use of a standard letter should also enable efficient preparation of the banks' replies.

It is common for banks to add a disclaimer at the end of their reply. Counsel's opinion is that the disclaimer does *not* significantly impair the value of the information given as audit evidence.

The main procedures are as follows.

- A standard letter should be sent in duplicate on each occasion by the auditor on his own note paper to each bank branch that the client holds an account at or has had dealings with since the end of the previous accounting period including where accounts closed during the period

- Auditors should ensure that the bank receives the client's authority to permit disclosure

- Letter should be sent two weeks in advance of the date of the client's year-end to enable the bank to provide the information within a reasonable time after the year end

- Dates entered on the standard letter are normally the closing dates of:
  o Client's current accounting period
  o Client's previous accounting period

- Auditors should ensure when reviewing the bank's reply that all questions have been answered in full

- Authenticity of any letters not received directly from the bank concerned, or for which the auditor has not made a previous request, must be checked

The information requested in the standard letter is as follows.

- *Bank accounts*
  - Details of all accounts with the bank and whether the balance is in favour of the bank or the customer
  - Details of accounts closed during the period
- *Accrued charges*
  - Amounts not yet charged or credited relating to fees and interest
  - Total interest charged for the period if not shown separately on statements
- *Set-off:* details of set-off arrangements (including those where there is no written arrangement)
- *Loans and other facilities*
  - Overdrafts and loans repayable on demand
  - Other loans specifying dates of review and repayment
- *Customers' assets held as security:* whether or not formally charged (and nature of charge or interest therein)
- *Customers' other assets* held: share certificates, title deeds and any other items
- *Contingent liabilities*
  - Bills discounted with recourse
  - Any guarantees, bonds or indemnities given to the bank by the customer on behalf of third parties
  - Outstanding forward foreign exchange contracts
- Other banks or branches where the customer has established a relationship during the period

**Creditors and accruals**

The objectives, with examples of relevant tests, are as follows.

*Completeness*

- Review creditors analytically compared to last year/budget
- Review GRNs around y/e: purchases correctly treated
- Review unpaid invoice files for liabilities not provided
- Review after date payment for liabilities not recorded
- Obtain a list of creditors and reconcile to the FS

*Ownership*

- Circularise trade creditors
- Reconcile balance at year end to suppliers' statements

Both these tests also provide evidence of completeness and valuation.

*Valuation*

Ensure closing provisions/accruals calculated in accordance with accounting policies and are consistent.

*Existence*

- Circularise/suppliers' statements
- Cut-off tests: purchases/credit notes

*Disclosure*

Ensure creditors properly analysed between those due in less than one year and those due in more than one year.

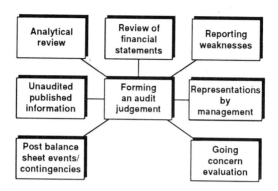

## Review of financial statements

An auditing guideline covers this area. The auditor must carry out a review to determine the following.

- Financial statements prepared using acceptable accounting policies, consistently applied and appropriate to enterprise

- Information included in financial statements is all internally consistent

- Adequate disclosure and proper classification and presentation of information

- Financial statements comply with statutory requirements and other regulations

- Review along with conclusions drawn from other tests, enables him to form an opinion on the financial statements

Accounting policies should:

- Comply with SSAPs or be otherwise acceptable
- Be consistent with those of previous periods
- Be consistently applied throughout the enterprise

## Analytical review

*Definition and explanation*

The term 'analytical review' is used to describe a variety of audit procedures, and encompasses the following.

- Analysing the relationship between items of financial data (eg sales and cost of sales), or between financial and non-financial information (eg payroll costs and size of the workforce)

- Comparing actual data with predictions derived from the analysis of known or expected relationships between items of data

- Comparing information for the latest period with corresponding information for earlier periods, other comparable enterprises or industry averages

- Investigating unexpected variations which are identified by such analysis and comparison

- Obtaining and substantiating explanations for those variations

- Evaluating the results of such analysis, comparison and investigation in the light of other audit evidence obtained to support the auditor's opinion on the financial statements

AR procedures range from simple comparisons to very sophisticated methods using computer audit software and advanced statistical techniques.

*Factors determining extent of use*

- The auditor needs to consider:
  - o Nature of enterprise
  - o Knowledge of client, and similar audits

- ○ Availability of information
- ○ Reliability, relevance, comparability and independence of information
- ○ Cost-effectiveness

- May be applied to:
  - ○ Individual account areas (eg sales)
  - ○ Financial information of enterprises
  - ○ Financial information on group accounts

- The procedure is particularly useful in diversified enterprises; it should be applied to financial information on individual business segments

*Procedures*

- The application of the technique is a four-stage process.
  - ○ Identify factors likely to have a material effect on items in the financial statements
  - ○ Ascertain the probable relationship between these factors and such items
  - ○ Predict the likely range of values of individual items
  - ○ Compare the prediction with actual recorded amounts

- Management explanations should be · obtained for significant fluctuations and corroborated by independent evidence

- If management perform AR procedures, the auditor should consider whether the approach, the data used and the results obtained are relevant for audit purposes

*Timing and objectives*

Use of AR generally depends upon the stage of the audit at which it is performed.

- *Planning stage*: consider preparatory procedures (eg assess the effect of changes in legislation; review interim/management accounts); the aims at this stage are:

  o  To improve the auditor's understanding of the enterprise

  o  To identify areas of the financial statements where the recorded values may vary from the expected values

  If variations are found, the auditor should conduct further work to discover their cause; and consider non-financial data and external factors

- *Detailed testing stage*

  o  AR is audit evidence; it is a form of substantive testing

  o  In *most* cases AR will be used in conjunction with other substantive tests

  o  AR procedures are a very effective means of testing for understatement

  o  Auditor must assess the level of assurance to be obtained, and this includes the following:

    –  Relevance, reliability, comparability and independence of data used

    –  Adequacy of controls over the preparation of internal information

    –  Accuracy with which figures being examined can be predicted

    –  Materiality of items

  o  Where explanations received for material unexpected variations cannot be substantiated, sufficient audit evidence must be obtained by other means

  o  If other evidence is not available, the auditor must consider qualifying his audit opinion; or, if the results of the AR reveal material error(s) then qualification must be considered

- *Review of financial statements stage*

  To support conclusions from other audit work, and to assess overall reasonableness of financial statements.

*Recording work done*

- Results of AR should be properly documented, and the auditor should compile a client profile in the permanent file detailing key ratios and trends from year to year

- AR should never be regarded as a mechanical process; it requires judgement, experience and a thorough knowledge of the business

## Unaudited published information

The auditing guideline *Financial information issued with audited financial statements* covers this area. The main aim is to ensure that the credibility of the financial statements is not undermined by other financial information published in the annual report. Only the directors' report is of importance.

*Statutory responsibilities*

If directors' report *inconsistent:*

- S 235 CA 1985: auditor's duty to consider whether information in directors' report is consistent with the accounts for the year and report if not consistent

- Possible inconsistencies:
  - Between actual figures or narrative
  - Between bases of preparation (if no disclosure of different bases)
  - Between figures and narrative interpretation of those figures

- Where inconsistencies discovered
  - o Discuss with directors to achieve elimination (including written communication if necessary)
  - o If not eliminated:
    - − If DR incorrect, 'refer to' in audit report (see below)
    - − If FS incorrect (unlikely), 'qualify' audit report

*Non-statutory responsibilities*

If directors' report misleading or other information inconsistent/misleading:

- Review all other financial information published as part of, or with, the annual report; may undermine the credibility of the audited financial statements if misleading/inconsistent

- Auditor should urge company not to publish annual report until after review completed

- If other information is inconsistent/misleading (or DR misleading)
  - o Discuss with directors to achieve elimination (including written communication to all directors if necessary)
  - o If not eliminated (and matter is potentially so misleading that it would be inappropriate for auditor to remain silent)
    - − Seek legal and professional advice
    - − Consider reference to matter in audit report*
    - − Consider exercising right under s 390 to be heard at GM

    * *Note.* There is no requirement for auditor to comment and the qualified privilege (ie defence to an action for defamation) may not extend to such comments

## Post balance sheet events/contingencies

*SSAP 17*

- *Post balance sheet events*: events, both favourable and unfavourable, which occur between the balance sheet date and the date on which the financial statements are approved by the board of directors

- The date on which the financial statements are approved by the board of directors is the date the board of directors formally approves a set of documents as the financial statements

- There are two types of post balance sheet events:
  - *Adjusting events* are PSBEs which provide additional evidence of conditions existing at the balance sheet date
  - *Non-adjusting events* are PSBEs which concern conditions which did not exist at the balance sheet date

Accounting treatment of PBSEs is as follows.

- Financial statements should be prepared on the basis of conditions existing at the balance sheet date

- *Adjusting PBSE*: amounts included in the financial statements should be changed

- *Non-adjusting PBSE*: disclose if of significant materiality:
  - Nature of the event
  - Estimate of the financial effect (if possible)

- Estimate of the financial effect disclosed before taking account of taxation, and taxation implications should be explained where necessary

- Date on which the financial statements were approved by the board should be disclosed

- Reversal or maturity of any window-dressing transactions should be disclosed

*Auditing guideline*

The dating of the audit report is:

- Normally date of actual signing

- Never earlier than date directors approve the financial statements but should be as close as possible to that date

The auditor's responsibilities in respect of PBSEs are as follows.

- Up to *date of the audit report*: auditor should take steps to obtain 'reasonable assurance' in respect of all significant events, so full PBSE review up to date of audit report

- From *audit report date to AGM:*
  - No duty to search for PBSEs
  - But, if becomes aware of information which might have led to a different opinion had he possessed it at the date of his report, then:
    - Discuss with directors
    - If directors unwilling to take necessary action, consider exercising rights under s 390 and take legal advice

- *After AGM*: if becomes aware of information which suggests that the financial statements are *wrong*:
  - Inform directors
  - If directors do not deal with correctly, consider taking legal advice

A specific audit programme to identify PBSEs would be as follows.

- Review results of normal year end audit work

- Consider adequacy of procedures taken by management to identify PBSEs

- Review any accounting records, management accounts for post balance sheet period

- Obtain profit forecasts, budgets, cash flow projections for post balance sheet period

- Review minutes of directors', management, special committee meetings

- Follow up on contingencies identified during the audit

- Consider effects of any other information which comes to light (eg newspaper reports)

## SSAP 18

*Contingency* is a condition which exists at the balance sheet date, where the outcome will be confirmed only on the occurrence or non-occurrence of one or more uncertain future events. A contingent gain or loss is a gain or loss dependent on a contingency.

The accounting treatment is as follows.

|  | *Contingent asset* | *Contingent liability* |
|---|---|---|
| Remote | No disclosure | No disclosure |
| Possible/probable | No disclosure | Disclosure |
| Highly probable | Disclosure | Provision |
| Virtually certain | Accrual | Provision |

Disclosure should be made as follows.

- Nature of the contingency

- Uncertainties which are expected to affect the ultimate outcome

- Prudent estimate of the financial effect, or a statement that it is not practicable to make such an estimate

- Where there is disclosure of an estimate of the financial effect of a contingency, the amount disclosed should be the potential financial effect; in the case of a contingent loss, this should be reduced by:

    o Any amounts accrued, and

    o Amounts of any components where the possibility of loss is remote

    The net amount only need be disclosed

The estimate of the financial effect should be disclosed before taking account of taxation, and the taxation implication of a contingency crystallising should be explained where necessary for a proper understanding of the financial position.

The following audit work should be performed.

- Obtain client's listing of contingencies

- Review client's system for identifying contingencies

- Review minutes of meetings of Board, key committees etc

- Examine correspondence eg solicitors, customers, suppliers, insurance company, banks etc

- Consider bills from solicitors - why incurred?

- Solicitor's letter

- Review contingencies from last year, are they still applicable?

- Consider nature of client's business - any likely contingencies eg warranty claims

- Review confirmation letter

- Obtain letter of representation from the directors

## Going concern evaluation

A new SAS covers this area: SAS 130 *The going concern basis in financial statements.*

### SSAP 2 definition

The enterprise will continue in operational existence for the foreseeable future .... assumes no intention or necessity to liquidate or curtail significantly the scale of operation.

### Foreseeable future

The new SAS does not define this, other than to state that if the directors have considered a period of less than one year from the date the FS are approved, the auditors should disclose this fact in their opinion.

### Prior indications of going concern problems

The SAS gives the following examples.

- *Financial*
    - An excess of liabilities over assets
    - Net current liabilities
    - Necessary borrowing facilities not agreed
    - Default on terms of loan agreements; potential breaches of convenant
    - Significant liquidity or cash flow problems
    - Major losses or cash flow problems since B/S date which threaten entity's existence

- o Substantial sales of fixed assets not intended to be replaced
- o Major restructuring of debts
- o Denial of (or reduction in) normal terms of trade credit by suppliers
- o Major debt repayment falling due where refinancing is necessary to the entity's continued existence
- o Inability to pay debts as they fall due

- *Operational*
  - o Fundamental changes to the market or technology to which the entity is unable to adapt adequately
  - o Externally forced reductions in operations (for example, as a result of legislation or regulatory action)
  - o Loss of key management or staff, labour difficulties or excessive dependence on a few product lines where the market is depressed
  - o Loss of key suppliers or customers or technical developments which render a key product obsolete

- *Other*
  - o Major litigation in which an adverse judgement would imperil the entity's continued existence
  - o Issues which involve a range of possible outcomes so wide that an unfavourable result could affect the appropriateness of the going concern basis

### Audit procedures

These should continue up to the date of the audit report.

- Review interim accounts/management information/budgets
- Review correspondence with customers, suppliers, bank
- Consult management about future intentions

- If evidence suggests that company may be unable to continue in business, review counter-balancing factors

- Review cash flow forecasts/budgets:
  o Compare to loan facilities
  o Perform tests of reasonableness/sensitivity analysis.

Possibly, obtain written evidence from client of steps to correct 'decline in fortunes'.

*Audit report*

- Possible unqualified opinion with added emphasis if auditor satisfied that going concern basis is appropriate

- 'Except for... might' if uncertainty is material

- 'Disclaimer' if uncertainty is fundamental

*Note*. Judge 'materiality' in terms of extent of adjustments that would need to be made to the FS if non-going concern.

## Representations by management

*CA 1985*

An officer of a company commits an offence if he knowingly or recklessly makes to the company's auditors a statement (whether written or oral) which is misleading, false or deceptive in a material particular (s 389A)

*Audit evidence*

- An auditor should not rely solely on unsupported oral representations by management as being sufficient reliable evidence

- Documentary evidence is more reliable than audit evidence

*Purpose of letter of representation*

- Written record of uncorroborated representations

- Ensures no misunderstanding as to information/ opinion/identity/authority

- Reminds directors of their responsibilities where the auditor prepares the accounts

*Audit procedures*

- Agree procedures at early stage (letter of engagement)

- Discuss letter with client first

- Signed by MD/FD on behalf of board

- Should be minuted

- Dated: after all other audit work completed but before signing of audit report

*Contents*

Restrict to matters where auditor *unable* to obtain independent corroborative evidence and could not reasonably expect it to be available.

- Where knowledge of facts confined to management
- Where matter is principally one of judgement

*If client refuses to sign*

- Auditor should write letter setting out his understanding and ask for management confirmation

- If management does not reply, auditor should follow up to ascertain his understanding is correct

- Auditor may conclude that he has not obtained sufficient information and explanations, in which case qualify

## Reporting weaknesses

This area is covered by an auditing guideline *Reports to management*

*Purposes*

- Communicate weaknesses/errors in system

- Give constructive advice eg improved efficiency

- Written record: may provide measure of protection where subsequent errors/defalcations

*Planning*

- Refer to report in engagement letter

- Timing: as soon a possible after the audit procedures giving rise to comment: both interim and final

*Contents*

- Weaknesses in systems

- Deficiencies in operation of systems

- Unsuitable accounting policies

- Non-compliance with SSAPs/ legislation

} State problem
Give egs
Outline
consequences
Make
recommendations

- State that letter is not necessarily comprehensive statement of all weaknesses etc

- State that letter is 'for private use' of client (to minimise liability)

- Request reply stating management action to be taken

*Procedures*

- Discuss with client to ensure factual accuracy and also recommendations are workable

- (Usually) address to board of directors

- Follow up reply

---

*Exam hint.* Many of the procedures covered in this chapter will be performed at about the same time, towards the end of an audit, so you may be asked about more than one in a question. *Do not* confuse the objectives or required audit work for each one.

---

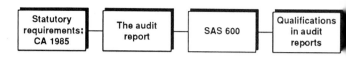

We looked at the unqualified audit report etc in Chapter 4; go back and look at the report.

## Statutory requirements: CA 1985

*S 235 Auditors' report*

A company's auditors must make a report to its members on the accounts examined by them, stating the following.

- Whether in the auditors' opinion the balance sheet and P&L a/c have been properly prepared in accordance with the Act

- Whether in their opinion a true and fair view is given:
  - In the balance sheet, of the state of the company's affairs at the end of the year
  - In the P&L a/c, of the company's profit or loss for the financial year
  - In the case of group accounts, of the state of affairs and profit or loss of the company and its subsidiaries dealt within by those accounts, so far as concerns members of the company

- If the information given in the directors' report is inconsistent with the accounts

*S 236 Signature of auditors' report*

The auditors' report must state the names of the auditors and be signed by them.

- Every audit report laid before the members at general meeting, published or circulated must state the names of the auditors

- The copy sent to the Registrar must state the names of the auditors and be signed by them

*S 237 Auditors' duties and powers*

Unless expressly mentioned in the auditors' report, the following will be implied.

- Proper accounting records have been kept by the company and proper returns adequate for the audit received from branches not visited

- The company's balance sheet and P&L a/c are in agreement with these

- The auditor has obtained all necessary information and explanations

- The disclosure requirements of:
  - Schedule 6
  - Part I Directors' emoluments
  - Parts II and III Loans and transactions with directors and officers

  have been complied with; if not, the auditors must include a statement giving the required particulars in their report

This section also gives the auditors the right to receive all information and explanations they think necessary.

*S 387A Rights to information*

- The auditors have a right of access at all times to the company's books, accounts and vouchers, and are entitled to require from the company's officers such information and explanations as they think necessary for the performance of their duties as auditors

- If an officer of a company knowingly or recklessly makes a false statement to a company's auditors, it is an offence, punishable by imprisonment, fine or both

## SAS 600

Go back to Chapter 4 and re-examine the audit report contents and format, as well as the statement of directors' responsibilities.

## Qualifications in audit reports

*Types of circumstance*

- *Uncertainty:* due to limitation on the scope of the auditors' examination

- *Disagreement*
  - Non-compliance with Companies Act
  - Non-compliance with SSAPs/FRSs
  - Disagreement due to known facts
  - Inadequate disclosure by the directors of inherent uncertainties and assumptions made in the preparation of the financial statements

*Two degrees of qualification*

- *Material,* but not fundamental

- *Fundamental*
  - For uncertainty, could make the accounts misleading (and therefore meaningless)
  - For disagreement, makes the accounts misleading: the financial statements do not give a true and fair view

*Qualification matrix*

| Nature of circumstances | Material | Fundamental |
| --- | --- | --- |
| Uncertainty | 'Except for .. might' | Disclaimer |
| Disagreement | 'Except for' | Adverse |

*Disagreement on accounting treatment/disclosure*

Where the auditors disagree with the accounting treatment or disclosure of a matter in the financial statements, and in the auditors' opinion the effect of that disagreement is material to the financial statements:

- The auditors should include in the opinion section of their report
  - Description of all substantive factors giving rise to the disagreement
  - Their implications for the financial statements
  - Where practicable, a quantification of the effect on the financial statements

- When the auditors conclude that the effect of the matter giving rise to disagreement is so material or pervasive that the financial statements are seriously misleading, they should issue an adverse opinion

- In the case of other material disagreements, the auditors should issue a qualified opinion indicating that it is expressed *except for* the effects of the matter giving rise to the disagreement

*Limitation of audit scope*

When there has been a limitation on the scope of the auditors' work that prevents them from obtaining sufficient evidence to express an unqualified opinion:

- The auditors' report should include a description of the factors leading to the limitation, in the opinion section

- The auditors should issue a disclaimer of opinion when the possible effect of a limitation on scope is so material or pervasive that they are unable to express an opinion on the financial statements

- A qualified opinion should be issued when the effect of the limitation is not so material or pervasive as to require a disclaimer, and the wording of the opinion should indicate that it is qualified as to the possible adjustments to the financial statements that might have been determined to be necessary had the limitation not existed

In considering whether a limitation results in a lack of evidence necessary to form an opinion, auditors assess:

- The quantity and type of evidence which may reasonably be expected to be available to support the particular figure or disclosure in the financial statements, and

- The possible effect on the financial statements of the matter for which insufficient evidence is available; when the possible effect is, in the opinion of the auditors, material to the financial statements, there will be insufficient evidence to support an unqualified opinion

*Fundamental uncertainty*

- In forming their opinion on financial statements, auditors should consider whether the view given by the financial statements could be affected by inherent uncertainties which, in their opinion, are fundamental

- When an inherent uncertainty exists which:
    o  In the auditors' opinion is fundamental, and

   o  Is adequately accounted for and disclosed in the financial statements,

the auditors should include an explanatory paragraph referring to the fundamental uncertainty in the opinion section

- When adding an explanatory paragraph, auditors should use words which clearly indicate that their opinion on the financial statements is not qualified in respect of its contents

*Inherent uncertainty*

Inherent uncertainties about the outcome of future events frequently affect, to some degree, a wide range of components of the financial statements at the date they are approved.

- In forming an opinion, auditors take into account the adequacy of the accounting treatment, estimates and disclosures of inherent uncertainties in the light of evidence available at the date they express that opinion

- Inherent uncertainties are regarded as fundamental when they involve a significant level of concern about the validity of the going concern basis or other matters whose potential effect on the fundamental statements is unusually great

---

*Exam hint.* If you are asked for a qualified audit report in the exam, it is probably only the opinion paragraph which will be requested. *Learn* the *qualification matrix* so you can reproduce it in your answer plan and then consider what type of qualification is required.

---

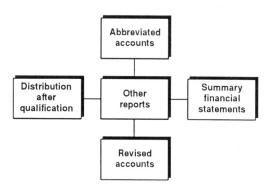

## Abbreviated accounts

CA 1985 allows certain companies defined as 'small' or 'medium-sized' to file an abbreviated set of accounts with the Registrar of Companies instead of the 'full accounts'.

*Defining criteria: s 246*

| Category | Criteria |
|---|---|
| Small | Turnover ≤ £2.8m |
| | *Balance sheet total ≤ £1.4m |
| | Average number of employees ≤ 50 |
| Medium-sized | Turnover ≤ £11.2m |
| | *Balance sheet total ≤ £5.6m |
| | Average number of employees ≤ 250 |

* Sum of all assets, without any deductions for liabilities

- All non-dormant companies must continue to prepare full accounts for presentation to shareholders and the exemptions only affect what is filed with the Registrar

- Excluded companies:
  - Plcs
  - Banking/insurance companies
  - Authorised under FSA 1986
  - Members of ineligible group

- Company must meet criteria in both current and previous year (unless new)

- Abbreviated accounts are not intended to give a true and fair view

*Small companies*

- File abbreviated version of normal B/S and certain notes

- Need *not* file P&L a/c, directors' report, emoluments of directors/higher paid employees, nor any disclosure required by SSAPs/FRSs

- B/S shows total amount for each category of asset/liability (letter/Roman numeral)

- Sch 4 CA 1985 still requires in the notes:
  - Accounting policies
  - Share capital
  - Particulars of allotments
  - Particulars of creditors payable < 5 years; security
  - Basis used in translating foreign currency into sterling

*Note.* A new set of 1992 regulations has allowed small companies to produce less information for their *full* accounts as well.

*Medium-sized companies*

- Accounts comprise full B/S, notes, directors' report plus *abbreviated* P&L a/c

- In P&L a/c combine turnover, cost of sales, gross P/L and other operating income under 'gross profit or loss'

- Omit note of analysis of turnover and P/L before tax

*Auditors' responsibilities*

- B/S must include, immediately above directors' signatures, a statement by the *directors* that they are entitled to file abbreviated accounts

- Before abbreviated accounts are filed, the auditors should consider whether, in their opinion, the conditions required for exemption have been satisfied

  o If not satisfied, the auditor must report this fact to the directors; the company could not produce abbreviated accounts

  o If satisfied, the auditor must prepare a 'special report' to this effect

- The special report:

  o Expresses the auditors' opinion that:

    – The directors are entitled to deliver abbreviated accounts as claimed in the directors' statement

    – The accounts have been 'properly prepared' in accordance with Sch 8 CA 1985

  o Includes the full text of the auditors' report under s 235

  o Should be addressed to the directors of the company

  o Will be delivered to the Registrar with the abbreviated accounts

- Ensure any qualification of full accounts does not affect any criteria for exemption

## Summary financial statements

Under s 251(1) CA 1985, plcs can issue SFS to members instead of full report.

- The SFS must be accompanied by a statement from the company's auditors which states that:
  - SFS consistent with the annual accounts and the directors' report
  - SFS comply with s 251 CA 1985 and the regulations made under that section

- The auditors' procedures in relation to the SFS will primarily be directed towards consideration of these two points.

- Where an inconsistency is found, if discussion with management does not result in the elimination of the inconsistency, the auditors should qualify their statement under s 251(4)(b), referring to the inconsistency

- If the auditors' report on the annual accounts was qualified, or if it included a statement under s 237(2) or (3) (for example that proper accounting records were not kept), the qualified report or statement is required to be set out in full in the SFS

## Revised accounts

To deal with accounts discovered to be defective *after* laying and delivering.

Previously there was no way to correct defective accounts. The form of revised accounts and reports are covered by the Companies (Revision of Defective Accounts and Report) Regulations 1990.

- Revision may be voluntary or by court order, due to non-compliance with the Act; voluntary revision of the accounts or the report under s 245 is not obligatory

- Use of hindsight limited, in determining whether accounts failed to comply with the Act, to events that took place *before* the accounts were approved (so estimates left unless based on fundamental errors)

- The revision of the accounts or directors' report may be undertaken by:
  o *Revision by replacement*, replacing the original with a new set of accounts or report or
  o *Revision by supplementary note*

*Audit procedures*

- No duty to search for defects after report signed

- If comes to attention of auditors, discuss with directors, take legal opinion etc

The following procedures should be undertaken.

- Review original audit plans in the light of the matter leading to revision and consider the extent to which additional audit evidence is required

- Reassess the various matters of judgement involved in the preparation of the original accounts

- Obtain evidence specific to the adjustments made to the original accounts

- Review the period after the date on which the original accounts were approved

- Review the revised accounts to give a reasonable basis for the auditors' opinion on the accounts

- Consider any legal and regulatory consequences of the revision

## Distribution after qualification

Under the CA 1985, companies whose accounts have been qualified may only make a distribution (pay a dividend) under certain circumstances.

- S 270: refer to 'relevant accounts', normally latest audited annual accounts

- S 271: if accounts qualified, auditor must state in writing whether the subject matter of the qualification is material in determining whether a dividend can be paid

- An *ultra vires* dividend can be recovered; negligence claims against auditors

- Auditor must be assured that the proposed distribution will be made out of profits available for that purpose: accumulated realised profits less accumulated realised losses not previously written off.

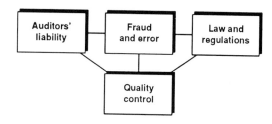

## Auditors' liability

Fundamental to the auditor's consideration of risk is the possibility that the auditor can be sued by the client under contract law (professional negligence, failure to spot a material employee fraud etc) or by a third party in tort.

As set out below a successful plaintiff must show that a duty of care was owed to him, and this duty was breached and a direct financial loss was suffered.

- Recent cases (*Caparo*, *Al Saudi Banque*) have narrowed the 'duty of care' considerably

- The *Littlejohn* case is a good example of how the auditor's duty is satisfied by a thorough well documented audit, in accordance with Auditing Standards

- Finally the *Jeb Fasteners* case remains pertinent in that it illustrates the principle of direct financial loss

*Possible courses of action*

An auditor can be sued for negligence in two ways.

- In *contract*: sued by the company/members: the auditor's contractual responsibilities are laid down in ss 235 and 237 CA 1985 and in the engagement letter

- *In tort*: sued by any other person who seeks to rely on the audited financial statements; a duty in tort exists where:
  - A duty of care is owed
    - Must be reasonably foreseeable that the statement/report would be relied upon
    - The relevant degree of proximity must exist
    - It must be just and reasonable to impose a duty of care on the defendant
  - There is a breach of that duty (ie negligence)
  - The plaintiff suffers a direct financial loss

A summary of key cases is as follows.

*Caparo Industries plc v Dickman & Others 1990*

In June 1984 Caparo made a successful bid for another plc, Fidelity, who were audited by Touche Ross. Having bought Fidelity, Caparo alleged that the auditors had been negligent. Caparo felt that reported pre-tax profits of £1.3m were, in reality, losses of £400,000. The issue that has finally been decided in the House of Lords is whether Touche Ross (in which D was a partner) owed a duty of care or not. Two 'relationships' were advanced by Caparo.

- At the year end and on the day Touche Ross signed the audit report, Caparo held a small shareholding in Fidelity

- Subsequently Caparo made a full bid relying on the audited accounts in their investment decision-making

*Held*: the auditor owes a responsibility to the company/shareholders as a whole, not to individual shareholders. Nor was there sufficient proximity between the auditors and Caparo as investors.

*Al Saudi Banque & Others v Clark Pixley 1989*

10 banks lent money to Gallic Credit Ltd, an import-export company. Of the 10 banks, 7 were creditors at the year-end, and 3 went on to lend money subsequently. The company's assets largely comprised of bills of exchange accepted by customers and drawn in Gallic's favour. The banks alleged that a large part of the company's business was fraudulent - the bills of exchange were not supported by underlying transactions and effectively new borrowing was being used to repay earlier loans. The company was compulsorily wound up with a deficiency for unsecured creditors estimated at £8.6m.

Although the alleged facts looked a little bleak for the auditors this case also foundered on the issue of *duty of care*.

*Held:*

- No duty was owed to the 3 banks because there was insufficient proximity

- No duty of care was owed to the 7 banks either - the auditors did not report to them; the banks did not appoint the auditors

*Littlejohn v Lloyd Cheyham 1985*

Plaintiff alleged auditor of trailer rental business had been negligent. Claimed had failed to consider tyre replacement policy: cash rather than accruals basis.

Audit client had gone into receivership a few months after the plaintiff had bought controlling interest.

Auditor's defence: had fully considered and documented tyre policy, including raising it in management letter. Also had issued going concern qualification and generally carried out a thorough audit.

*Held*: thorough audit (per auditing standards) is a good defence against claims of negligence.

### Jeb Fasteners Ltd v Marks Bloom & Co 1980

Jeb acquired entire share capital of another company, suffered substantial loss and sued Marks Bloom who had audited the company's account on which they had relied.

*Held*: duty of care owed by auditors to plaintiff, even though they didn't know of his existence, or that any takeover bid was being planned.

Mr Justice Woolf held the appropriate test was whether the auditor knew or reasonably should have foreseen at the time at which the account were audited, that a person might rely on them for the purpose of deciding whether or not to take over the company and could therefore suffer loss if the accounts were inaccurate.

In this pre-*Caparo* case the judge decided there was a duty of care but Marks Bloom 'got off' because their client would have been bought anyway - it was bought for its management rather than its (negligently) audited balance sheet.

### Summary of current position

Recent case law has narrowed the liability of auditors towards 3rd parties who rely on the audited accounts.

*House of Lords decision*: 'The purpose of the (audit report is) to provide those entitled to it with information to enable them to exercise their proprietary powers ... (it is) not for individual speculation with a view to profit': this is at odds with commercial reality and CA 1985.

*Commercial reality* is that creditors and investors (especially institutional ones) *do* use audited accounts. S 241 CA 1985 requires a company to file accounts with the Registrar. Why is this a statutory requirement? Surely because the public including creditors and potential investors have a need for a credible and independent view of the company's performance and position.

It would be unjust if auditors, who have secondary responsibility for financial statements being prepared negligently, bore the full responsibility for losses arising from such negligence just because they are insured.

It would also be unjust if the auditor could be sued by all and sundry. While the profession have generally welcomed *Caparo* two obvious problems are raised by decision.

- Is a restricted view of the usefulness of audited accounts in the profession's long-term interest?

- For private companies there will probably be an increase in the incidence of personal guarantees and warranties given by the directors to banks and suppliers

**Fraud and error**

Auditing guideline *The auditor's responsibility in relation to fraud, other irregularities and errors.*

*General background*

Covers *illegal acts* in general as well as *fraud and irregularities*.

- *Error*: unintentional misstatement in accounting records/ financial statements

- *Irregularity*: intentional misstatements and misappropriation of assets

- *Fraud*: irregularities involving the use of criminal deception to obtain an unjust or illegal advantage

- *Illegal act*: act/transaction entered in name of client, contrary to law - intentionally or inadvertently

The auditors should plan their audit with reasonable expectation of detecting material misstatements in the financial statements, whether they are caused by fraud, other irregularities or errors.

*Responsibilities for detection of improprieties*

- Responsibility for prevention and primary responsibility detection lies with management

- Statutory provisions covering management responsibilities:
  - CA 1985: proper accounting records; prepare accounts
  - Theft Act 1968: false accounting
  - Insolvency Act 1986: wrongful trading

- Auditors should remind management of their responsibilities

- Auditors have duty to act with skill and care exercised by reasonably competent auditor in particular circumstances; judged by reference to standards generally applied by accountancy profession for proper competent conduct of audit

- Auditors' responsibility toward irregularities and errors is to design work with reasonable expectation of detecting those which might impair truth and fairness of financial statements

*Planning*

- Assessment of risk that material irregularity, error or breach of directly relevant legislation could occur
  - Business environment eg assets readily susceptible to misappropriation
  - Control environment

- In reaching their decision as to the areas to be tested and number of balances and transactions to examine, auditors will consider information available from prior experience, knowledge of client

- For detection of material irregularities, errors and breaches of legislation, auditor will consider:
  - Extent of legislation
  - Risk that irregularities etc may impair true and fair view
  - Risk that such items remain undetected by company
  - Relative effectiveness of different audit tests

- Procedures should be adopted to assess clients' compliance with directly relevant legislation eg CA 1985: review directors' loan accounts

- Many potential illegal acts will only rarely come to auditors' attention in course of work eg breach of employment legislation

- Not practical for auditors to plan work with such legislation specifically in mind, but may become aware of them

- Circumstances indicative of improprieties:
  - Lack of records/control breakdowns: missing/falsified vouchers/documents; unauthorised transactions
  - Unsatisfactory explanations: reconciliations/suspense accounts; AR
  - Payments: penalties/fines; commissions; to government officials
  - Others: investigations by government departments, police; unduly lavish lifestyles by officers, employees

- Many tests normally performed by auditors may assist in isolating improprieties eg debtors testing may reveal 'teeming and lading'

- Action to be taken on discovery of an impropriety:
  - Additional tests
  - Consider nature, cause and likely effect on FS
  - Discuss with management to keep informed/rectify
  - Consider likely recurrence
  - Take legal advice

*Reporting to management*

- If appropriate, report should be made to board of directors/audit committee

- If management involved, ensure senior level informed

- Legal advice if auditor believes report may not be acted on

- Make recommendations of good practice to help prevent further occurrences

*Reporting to shareholders*

- No specific responsibility to report on impropriety in audit report if financial statements give a true and fair view

- Notwithstanding materiality, the auditors may be required to report under other reporting responsibilities

- If auditors consider they have been prevented from executing their work to such an extent that they are unable to report, they should resign, making reasons known

*Reporting to third parties*

- Normally, duty of confidentiality prevents reporting without client's permission

- Not bound if criminal offence and ordered by court or government officer

- May obtain legal advice as to whether duty of confidentiality should be disregarded

- Consider:
  - Extent to which members of public will be affected
  - Gravity
  - Relative size of amounts
  - Reasons for client's unwillingness to disclose
  - Likely repetition

- May be appropriate to bring to attention of regulatory authorities (eg FSA 1986 s 109)
  - Weakness in system control/accounting records
  - Fraud by senior management

- Except where inappropriate that matter be drawn to attention of directors, auditors should request management to disclose and only use right to report if request not complied with

- The auditors should ensure any decision to report would stand up to examination at a future date

---

*Exam hint.* The APB has just produced two new SASs on *Fraud and error* and *Consideration of law and regulations*. These are not yet examinable, but may become so in the near future.

---

## Quality control

Quality control has already been mentioned in previous chapters. The auditing guideline *Quality control* sets out procedures which can be adopted by the firm to ensure all work is properly controlled.

Each firm should establish procedures appropriate to its circumstances and communicate them to all partners and relevant staff. This normally involves putting them in writing, although oral communication may be effective in the small, closely controlled firm.

*Acceptance of appointment/reappointment*

Consider the firm's own independence and its ability to provide an adequate service to the client.

*Professional ethics*

Ensure all partners and professional staff adhere to the principles of independence, objectivity, integrity and confidentiality, as set out by the ACCA.

*Skills and competence*

- *Recruit* personnel with right qualifications

- *Training* should be used to keep staff updated:
  - Circulate digests/texts etc
  - Maintain technical library
  - Issue technical circulars/memos
  - Encourage training courses
  - Maintain training arrangements

  Will vary from firm to firm

- *On-the-job-training* covering different types of work, properly supervised with evaluations of performance

- Staff should be informed of the firm's procedures, for example by means of manuals and standardised documentation or programmes; regularly updated

*Consultation*

- Structured review of audit files
- Refer technical queries to specialist
- Procedures to resolve judgemental matters
- Monitoring the firm's procedures

*Monitoring the firm's procedures*

Quality control procedures (as above) should be monitored constantly, with periodic review of a sample of audit files by independent reviewers in the firm; this is not to control the audit, but assess quality control. Smaller firms use other firms or advisory service.

---

*Exam hint.* Although it is important to learn about other cases to understand auditor liability, the key case here is *Caparo*: make sure you understand its ramifications.

---

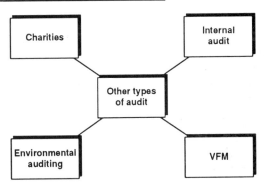

## Internal audit

According to the auditing guideline *Reliance on internal audit* the external auditor should make a general assessment of IA to determine whether to place reliance thereon.

*External vs internal auditor*

- *External auditor*
  - o *Objectives*
    - – Opinion on FS in true and fair terms
    - – Proper accounting records etc
  - o *Reports* to members
- *Internal auditor*
  - o *Objectives* up to employer, may include:
    - – Review accounting systems and controls
    - – Examine financial/operating information
    - – VFM
    - – Implementation of corporate policies

  –   Special investigations
  o   *Reports* to management

*Reliability of internal audit*

If the auditors are thinking of using the internal auditors they must first make a general assessment of them.

*General assessment* includes:

- Degree of independence
- Scope and objectives
- Due professional care
- Technical competence
- Internal audit reports
- Level of resources available

*Extent of reliance*: factors to consider include:

- Materiality of areas
- Audit risk inherent
- Level of judgement
- Sufficiency of complementary evidence
- Specialist skills of internal audit staff

In planning, controlling and recording, the external auditors should:

- Liaise closely with the internal auditor at all stages
- Compare results with those produced by EA staff

External auditor should consider whether he should report separately to management any weaknesses/irregularities discovered by internal audit.

The external auditor cannot make reference to work done by the internal auditor in his statutory report.

## VFM

Value for money audits have generally been associated with the public sector, but can be carried out in any type of organisation.

VFM audits assess the 'three Es'.

- *Economy*: attaining the appropriate quantity and quality for physical, human and financial resources (inputs) at lowest cost

- *Efficiency*: optimum relationship between goods/services produced (outputs) and the resources used to produce them

- *Effectiveness*: concerned with how well an activity is achieving its policy objectives or other intended effects

In profit-making bodies objectives can be expressed financially in terms of 'profit' or 'return'. For not-for-profit organisations, non-monetary terms may be more appropriate, requiring comparison with alternative use of resources etc.

The auditor will carry out a VFM audit by looking at: *Inputs, Outputs, Impacts.*

## Environmental auditing

This is a very new area, but it is likely to become very important as businesses are made accountable for the impact they have on the environment (as is already the case in the USA).

Recent UK reports have looked at the following.

- Include an environmental report in the annual report

- Potential environmental liabilities should be disclosed, even if they are not a contingent liability per SSAP 18

- FRS should be produced with proper definitions of 'environment' etc, laying out the information to be disclosed

- Environmental issues should be integrated into all aspects of corporate management

A voluntary scheme for eco-audits has been set up by the European Commission. The *Eco-audit Scheme* aims to promote improvements in company environmental performance. Companies would register for the audit and then:

- Hold environmental audits
- Set up a framework for continuing appraisal
- Prepare periodic environmental statements per site

## Charities

Although this section only looks at charities, many of the principles can be applied to other non-profit making organisations, such as company nurseries, clubs, societies etc.

*Charity accounts*

The annual report of a charity should contain:

- Legal and administrative detail

- Trustee's report

- Accounts
  - Income and expenditure account (I&E a/c)
  - Balance sheet
  - Cash flow statement (SSAF)

*Problems with charity accounts and audits*

- *Cash income:* difficult to institute procedures to ensure that all cash collections properly accounted for in the books of

account; the cut-off date for the cash income of some
charities is not always the year-end date

- *Donations in kind:* charities are sometimes reluctant, or find
  it impracticable, to bring donations in kind into their books at
  their market value

- *Legacies:* legacy income fluctuates considerably, so
  charities frequently employ a legacy equalisation account

- *Specific funds*: charities may produce separate accounts to
  detail movements in certain funds for which they act as
  trustee or which represent monies raised for specific
  projects; categories of specific funds include designated,
  restricted and endowment funds

- *Central and local government grants and loans*: charities
  may be eligible for a number of grants and loans, which can
  create problems in respect of: knowing of the existence of
  the grant or loan scheme and the right to claim, *and* using
  the money for the correct purpose

*Internal controls*

Internal controls should be in place over:

- Donations from collecting boxes and tins
- Donations from post
- Deeds of covenant
- Legacies
- Fund-raising activities
- Central/local government grants/loans
- Branches
- Fixed assets and depreciation
- Specific funds
- Grants to beneficiaries
- Bank records

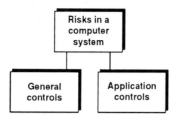

## Risks in computer systems

- Human error: data entry errors, command errors
- Technical error: failure of hardware or software
- Natural disaster: mainly fire and flood
- Deliberate action: fraud
- Commercial espionage
- Malicious damage: damage with no monetary gain
- Industrial action: over-reliance on key personnel

Two types of control are implemented to tackle these problems:

- General controls
- Application controls

## General controls

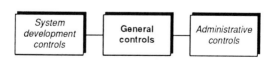

General controls are controls around the computer system to ensure it is operating in a secure environment. There are two types.

- *System development controls*: to ensure that the system in operation has been planned to meet the needs of the organisation and that there has been proper training and testing prior to implementation

- *Administrative controls*: to ensure that the operation of the system is efficient, controlled and properly supervised so that the system is operating smoothly and efficiently

## System development controls

- *Viruses*: need to ensure program and data files are not corrupted:
  - No unauthorised use of games software
  - Resident 'anti-virus software'
  - Vetting of all new files loaded onto the system

- *Small systems*: ensure the system purchased is appropriated to the task:
  - Define the objectives of the system and ensure those needs are met
  - Purchase from a reputable supplier
  - Review the available documentation
  - Assess the available training for staff
  - Assess the on-going financial viability of the supplier to ensure future support and development will be available
  - Enter maintenance contracts
  - Identify other users of that system and ask for their opinion of that system
  - Control the conversion of files from the old to the new system

- *Large systems*: ensure the internally developed system meets the organisation's needs:

- o Adopt a recognised and documented system analysis and design method
- o Full ongoing documentation throughout the development stages
- o Review and approval throughout development stages
- o Test data designed to impact on all system areas with pre-determined results
- o Full testing prior to implementation
- o Approval of system documentation with external auditors
- o Full training schemes set up
- o User documentation reviewed prior to implementation
- o Controlled file conversion from old to new system
- o Review ability of development staff

*Administrative controls*

- *Division of duties*: ensure staff functions are not incompatible:
  - o Restriction of access to program and data files using passwords and user identification; this restriction is often split into users who can access and change files and those who can access for enquiry only
  - o Organisation charts showing individuals and their responsibilities
  - o Locking keyboards when not in use

- *File control*: ensure the integrity of program and data files:
  - o Password protection and user IDs
  - o Regular backup and secure storage of files
  - o Periodic print-outs of files
  - o Secure storage procedures including labelling of storage devices and write/protect labels

- o Program files issued to programmers only with authorisation and acceptance of amended files for use only where all amendments have been properly authorised (larger systems)

- *Control over operators*: monitor and control the work of staff:
  - o Maintain operating logs showing when users have accessed the system and the files they used, preferably by exception
  - o Adequate training and supervision
  - o Job schedule to allow central control over when users have access

- *Physical security*: reduce the risk of hardware failure and minimise any resultant loss:
  - o Environmental controls, eg air conditioning
  - o Secure computer rooms (large systems)
  - o Fire precautions: fire detectors, extinguishers
  - o Maintenance agreements (usually a 24-hour repair or replace agreement)
  - o Standby agreements with either the users of similar systems or computer bureaux to use their systems in the event of failure

## Application controls

Application controls are controls 'within' the computer system to ensure that the transactions processed by the system result in information which is accurate, complete and valid.

*Input controls*

To ensure any data input onto the system is valid, accurate and complete:

- Batch controls where data entered onto the system is first subject to manual processes to pre-determine the results and the input data is only accepted when it meets the pre-determined totals; typically checked: no of documents; net amount; gross amount; hash totals for dates/codes

- Range/limit checks which specify maximum and minimum expected values

- Existence checks that will only allow data to be input for valid account codes

- Check digits which give codes a pattern; data will not be accepted for codes which do not match this pattern

- Sequence checks which will highlight gaps in data both within and between batches

### Controls over processing

To ensure processing is accurate and complete:

- Good systems development and security of program files
- Periodic running of test data
- Sequence checks during processing

### Output controls

To ensure the completeness and security of output:

- Independent review and investigation of error and exception reports; ensure corrections are followed up and resubmitted

- Batch controls to carry out control account reconciliations once processing is complete

- Use of sequence numbers

- Large systems: printers kept in a secure location and output register maintained, recording who received information